Church history is the story of God's providence worked out through the lives of His people. As Hebrews 11 demonstrates to us, we are meant to learn from faithful believers who have gone before us and who ever point us to Christ who is 'the author and perfecter of faith.' For this reason and more, I am a huge fan of well-written Christian biography. To that category, we now can add Jacob Tanner's *The Tinker's Progress*. Full of life, intrigue, and expressiveness, Tanner's biography on John Bunyan gives us an even-handed yet sympathetic treatment of one of Puritanism's most well-loved heroes. More than straight biography, however, Tanner sprinkles his offering with biblical and theological insights, as well as anecdotes from church history. The skillful weaving of all these elements together leaves us with a delightful and encouraging story of the beloved Tinker. Warmly recommended!

NATE PICKOWICZ
Teaching Pastor, Harvest Bible Church, Gilmanton Iron Works,
New Hampshire; author, *Christ & Creed*

The Tinker's Progress: The Life and Times of John Bunyan by Jacob Tanner introduces us afresh to the sustaining, saving, and shaping work of God's providential hand in the life of John Bunyan. This work provides insightful reflections on historical events used by God to produce one of my spiritual heroes. I highly commend this work to anyone who desires to get to know the man who gave us *The Pilgrims Progress* better.

GARRETT KELL
Pastor, Del Ray Baptist Church, Alexandria, Virginia

Perhaps no single pastor has shaped the Christian imagination more than John Bunyan, but few today know much about this tinker-turned-pastor. Jacob Tanner beautifully tells the story of Bunyan's life and ministry, allowing us to observe and be shaped by Bunyan's progress down the pilgrim's path. I highly recommend this book for all who desire to know John Bunyan better.

SCOTT ANIOL
Executive Vice President and Editor-in-Chief, G3 Ministries

John Bunyan was a man who was pierced to the heart with the Word. He was subsequently shaped by it because he was tested through persecution, suffering, and temptation. The light of Bunyan's work burns bright, not because of Bunyan himself, but because Christ was honored in his life and work. Today, we need Christian men and women of godly character who follow in the long line of men like Bunyan, who have gone before us and are grounded in and shaped by the Word and church history. The best Christian biographies highlight the life and theology of the subject, intending to help the reader understand more of the Scriptures and the glories of Christ in the pages therein. In his excellent book, *The Tinker's Progress: The Life and Times of John Bunyan,* Jacob Tanner has given the Church a great gift: a timeless treasure of Bunyan's life and ministry. I pray *The Tinker's Progress* will be read widely and encourage a new generation to read and study Bunyan's theology, thereby being shaped and molded by the Bible like Bunyan.

DAVE JENKINS
Executive Director, Servants of Grace Ministries

The Tinker's Progress is the kind of autobiography we need: brief, bold, and beautiful. Tanner walks you through the life of one of Christ's most precious saints exuberant enthusiasm that leave you feeling as if he was a dear friend of Bunyan's and just found out he was finally saved after years of prayer. So dive in with him, and learn of he grace abounding to the chief of sinners.

CHRIS MARLEY
Senior Pastor, Miller Valley Baptist Church, Prescott, Arizona

We need more, not less, of Bunyan. I read Spurgeon every day. To do so is to encounter Bunyan at almost every turn. I want to know Bunyan better, the man whose story and writings most influenced Spurgeon. We owe Jacob Tanner a debt of gratitude for his fresh work on Bunyan. Through this new book, Bunyan lives again.

RAY RHODES, JR.
Pastor, Grace Community Church, Dawsonville, Georgia;
author, *Susie: The Life and Legacy of Susannah Spurgeon*

THE TINKER'S PROGRESS

THE LIFE & TIMES OF JOHN BUNYAN

JACOB TANNER

CHRISTIAN
FOCUS

Copyright © Jacob Tanner 2024

hardback ISBN 978-1-5271-1006-9
ebook ISBN 978-1-5271-1122-6

10 9 8 7 6 5 4 3 2 1

Published in 2024
by
Christian Focus Publications Ltd,
Geanies House, Fearn, Ross-shire,
IV20 1TW, Great Britain.

www.christianfocus.com

Cover design by Daniel Van Straaten

Printed and bound by
Bell & Bain, Glasgow

Contents

For my sons, Josiah and Owen.

*May the Lord's grace abound in your own lives
as it did in the Tinker's
and may you both know the great joy
of serving Christ and His Kingdom.*

INTRODUCTION

'This hill, though high, I covet to ascend;
The difficulty will not me offend.
For I perceive the way to life lies here.
Come, pluck up, heart; let's neither faint nor fear.
Better, though difficult, the right way to go,
Than wrong, though easy, where the end is woe.'

(Christian, Ascending the Hill of Difficulty in
The Pilgrim's Progress)

I first encountered the Tinker and his writings when I was around ten years old. As a gift, I had received a children's edition of *The Pilgrim's Progress*. I dimly recall there being pictures of Christian making his journey, but the gist of the story was about all I learned at the time. I vaguely knew it was about a man who makes a journey to the eternal city that God has promised to all His faithful. But, in my young mind, I had confused John Bunyan with Paul Bunyan and mingled different stories together. I thought that Christian's story in *The Pilgrim's Progress* was somehow connected to the American legend of Paul Bunyan and Babe the Blue Ox.

My next encounter with John Bunyan would not come until a few years later, when I was in middle school. When I was thirteen, my homeschooling curriculum sent me an abridged edition of *The Pilgrim's Progress*. It was missing various portions of the text and had been updated and modernized for a twenty-first century context. But I liked what I read and wanted more. I sought a full, unabridged edition of the text and, since then, have worked my way through it on more than one occasion.

Within *Pilgrim's Progress*, I found a beautiful and poetic articulation of the Christian faith in allegorical form. Later, I read *Holy War*, and found another allegorical tale that rivals the works of a Dante or Milton. I have often thought that Bunyan does not get enough credit in this regard: He was a fabulous writer, and his allegorical tales and poems deserve the attention of a modern readership.

Literary scholars take the writings of men like Milton and Dante seriously. Many Christians today are familiar with J.R.R. Tolkien's *Middle-Earth*, and a great deal more with the allegorical stories of C.S. Lewis' *Narnia*. Sitting on my shelf, in 2021, I have at least four biographies on Tolkien and a few more on Lewis. I have books devoted entirely to exploring their fictional worlds and universes. While I do appreciate these authors and their writings, none of them have personally touched me in the way that Bunyan's writings have. However, it often appears to me, in passing, that Bunyan is not in these literary conversations. But, oh, how he deserves to be!

There was a time when Bunyan was a household name. In some ways, maybe he still is. *The Pilgrim's Progress* has sold over 250 million copies and has the potential to reach an even wider audience, being now available in the public domain. But I have noticed that it seems more likely these days that Christians have a greater knowledge of *The Lord of the Rings* rather than *Pilgrim's Progress*. Comparatively fewer still are familiar with *Holy War*, or the plethora of other writings from Bunyan.

This ought not to be so. Bunyan's own writings, though far different from a Tolkien or a Lewis, can stand shoulder to shoulder with either of those men's best works and, doctrinally speaking, are far greater. I typically preface my enjoyment of Lewis' or Tolkien's works with the statement, 'I enjoy their writings, their worlds, and their characters, but I generally would not seek to learn theology from them.' This preface is unnecessary with Bunyan. Especially within Reformed circles, Bunyan ought to be remembered, in my earnest opinion, as a writer par-excellence who matched Tolkien's and Lewis' technical abilities, and at times possessed a far greater understanding of Scripture and theology than either of them did.

Part of the reason, then, for my desire to write this biography of the Tinker is because I long to see him mentioned within the same conversations as Dante, Milton, Lewis, and Tolkien. When it comes to allegorical works, there is, in my humble estimation, none that God equipped more greatly than the Tinker. Among preachers, Bunyan ought to be remembered alongside the Chrysostoms and Spurgeons of the Lord's Church. Among the influential, Bunyan deserves recognition alongside the Augustines, Luthers, and Calvins. Among pious Christians, Bunyan ought to be named alongside the humblest and grace filled.

The point is this: Bunyan is so much *more* than a writer of allegory, so much *more* than a preacher, and so much *more* than a gifted pastor. He is not less than any of these things, but, when viewed as a whole, Bunyan rises as an example, imperfect though he was, of what a Christian ought to be.

Bunyan: Tinker and Thinker

After I rediscovered Bunyan in my teens, I sought out some of his other writings. One of the beauties of the twenty-first century is the ease of availability when it comes to the writings of the Puritans and Bunyan is no exception to this. Around age fourteen, I downloaded as many of his works as I could to my e-reader. I remember how shocked I was to find that, compared to many others, he was practically unlearned and uneducated—reading his writings would never reveal it! The occupation of humble Tinker must have confused many in his own day when they learned that he was also an incredible *Thinker*. That is to say, he was a gifted theologian and interpreter of Scripture.

In the preface to Bunyan's *Works*, George Offer writes that:

Of all the objections that have been made to Bunyan's works, the most absurd is, that he was poor and unlettered. To despise the poor is an impious reflection upon Divine wisdom. It is true that great grace can keep the scholar humble, and bless his learning to the welfare of the church, but for the welfare of the world we want many Bunyans, and can manage with few Preistleys or Porsons.

Bunyan, although unlearned as to the arts and sciences of this world, was deeply versed in the mysteries of godliness, and the glories of the world to come. He was a most truthful, ingenious, persuasive, and invaluable writer upon the essentials of human happiness. To refuse his Scriptural instruction, because he was not versed in chemistry, mathematics, Greek, or Latin, would be to proclaim ourselves void of understanding.[1]

Bunyan may have been uneducated in these finer points and, academically speaking, would fall woefully short of a John Owen. But when it came to practical and experiential mastery of the Scriptures and their theology, Bunyan was as gifted as they come. If it is true that a man cannot be said to have mastered material unless he is able to explain it in a simple way so that even young children can understand, then it also must be granted that Bunyan was an uneducated genius who understood Scripture with a certain amount of depth and clarity seldomly found in even the supreme theologians of our own day.

As I searched for and found Bunyan's other writings, I was continually impressed by the beauty and practicality of what he wrote and even the way he wrote. I had never really encountered any sort of Christian writing that combined beauty and practicality. Usually, if the prose was beautiful, the practicality of what I read was lacking. Purely practical writings, on the other hand, were seldom beautiful. Rarely did either sort move me to praise.

Not so with Bunyan. His writings, even now, almost always move me to doxological praise of our Triune God. He can, in the same paragraph, teach a great truth about God, offer a great exhortation and challenge to pursue holiness and piety

---

1. George Offer, *Preface* to *The Works of John Bunyan* (Edinburgh, UK: The Banner of Truth Trust, 1991), 1:vii.

in earnest, and then encourage and comfort the stumbling Christian. This is a rare talent even in modern writers and is an evidence of the indwelling of the Holy Spirit in the Tinker. Furthermore, as already stated above, his writing and preaching is a fantastic example of the Puritan spirit of Reformed, experiential theology. Bunyan, perhaps more than any other theologian, teaches that theology and doctrine are not to be reserved for stuffy academic halls or the rote machinations of armchair theologians. Theology and doctrine are practical for the Christian life and are meant to be understood and lived out. The greater the Christian's understanding of truth, the stronger their own passion for Jesus will be, and the greater their worship and doxology will become. Bunyan evidenced this in his own life, as I hope to show throughout this book, and then taught this truth to others.

The Tinker and the Twenty-First Century

If you've read this far, I truly hope that you will stick with this work. But you may be wondering: What can I learn in my modern context from a Puritan who lived nearly four centuries ago?

As it turns out, there is a great deal to learn from Bunyan. He can teach men how to be mature men, fathers how to be loving fathers, husbands how to be faithful husbands, pastors how to be tender pastors, suffering saints how to suffer well, and Christians how to be steadfast Christians. Yet, perhaps one of his greatest lessons to modern Christians is how one may live faithfully to Christ in a world that is antagonistic to God.

Bunyan was a Nonconformist and knew what it was to be persecuted for his faith. He knew the harsh reality of what it means to pick up the cross and follow Jesus. He had counted the cost and esteemed the riches of following Christ as greater than anything the world could ever offer, but personally experienced the reality of deep suffering for Christ. Like Moses before him, Bunyan lived his life, 'Choosing rather to suffer affliction with the people of God, than to enjoy the pleasures of sin for a season; Esteeming the reproach of Christ greater riches than the treasures in Egypt: for he had respect unto the recompence of the reward. By faith he forsook Egypt, not fearing the wrath of the king: for he endured, as seeing him who is invisible' (Heb. 11:25-27). Perhaps it would be better to say that in esteeming the reproach of Christ as greater riches than the treasures of this world, Bunyan forsook both his former life of sin and the ease of conforming to rules and laws that he saw as profoundly unbiblical.

It seems likely that many who will read this will have experienced suffering of one kind or another for the sake of Christ. It is also possible that some reading will have experienced a threat to stop preaching the gospel, and even witnessed governments outlawing the public assembling together of Christians on the Lord's Day. Others still may also read this work because they are seeking help for following Christ in the midst of extreme turmoil and persecution.

Knowing what I know of Bunyan through his writings, I think he would wholeheartedly endorse the statement, 'Obey God, Defy Tyrants.' In his own obedience to God, he was willing to be imprisoned and even refused release when given the ultimatum of freedom if he would just stop preaching. Such a spirit is peculiar to those Christians who are truly passionate about Christ, His glory, and His Kingdom. To receive the favor of men for rejection of Christ was not an option for the Tinker. His dignity was found within his total commitment to his sovereign Lord. The shame and reproach of the world he would gladly bear if it meant the glory of God.

It is often the case that *Pilgrim's Progress* sheds light on and provides insight into Bunyan's own state of mind. At one point, Christian meets another character named Faith. During this part of the story, Christian and Faith are conversing with one another and Christian asks Faith about Shame; the shame one may feel for following Christ when ridiculed by the world, the shame one may endure when harshly persecuted by sinners; the shame one may experience when all have abandoned them because of their faith in Christ. Faith responds:

> Therefore, thought I, what God says is best—is best, though all the men in the world are against it. Seeing, then, that God prefers His religion; seeing God prefers a tender conscience;

seeing they that make themselves fools for the kingdom of heaven are wisest, and that the poor man that loveth Christ is richer than the greatest man in the world that hates Him; Shame, depart! thou art an enemy to my salvation. Shall I listen to thee against my sovereign Lord? how, then, shall I look Him in the face at His coming? Should I now be ashamed of His way and servants how can I expect the blessing?[2]

Bunyan's own life is a testament to the strengthening power of faith against shame. Threatened, persecuted, arrested, and imprisoned, Bunyan never turned away his gaze from Christ. His writing, preaching, pastoring, and Christian resistance to tyranny were not manufactured fronts. This was who Bunyan was, both in public and behind closed doors. He was a man deeply committed to Christ, His Church, and the doctrines of Scripture. He can teach us today what it means to follow Christ and how a Christian can do so in the face of severe suffering.

A Hebrews 11 Sort of Christian

While certainly far from perfect, Bunyan is an example of what it means to be a Christian. His is a life that, when studied, reveals the necessity of God's grace to grow and mature in Christ. Just as Christian progresses in his journey in Bunyan's most famous story, Bunyan himself was a pilgrim progressing through the Christian life. I think Bunyan would be most pleased if, when examining his life, we would continually be redirected to Jesus Christ, who is the author and perfecter of our own faith.

In fact, I often imagine what the Hebrews 11 'Hall of Faith' might look like in the twenty-first century. I like to imagine it would include many of the Church Fathers like Athanasius and Augustine, Reformers like Luther and Calvin, and Puritans like Owen, Edwards, and, of course, Bunyan. These men stood boldly and courageously for Christ and His Kingdom, suffered well, and did all for the glory of God.

---

2. John Bunyan, *The Pilgrim's Progress*, *Works*, 3:120.

Hebrews 11:33-40 is clearly about those Old Testament saints who are mentioned in previous verses, but I think that they speak well of men like Bunyan as well:

> Who through faith subdued kingdoms, wrought righteousness, obtained promises, stopped the mouths of lions. Quenched the violence of fire, escaped the edge of the sword, out of weakness were made strong, waxed valiant in fight, turned to flight the armies of the aliens. Women received their dead raised to life again: and others were tortured, not accepting deliverance; that they might obtain a better resurrection: And others had trial of cruel mockings and scourgings, yea, moreover of bonds and imprisonment: They were stoned, they were sawn asunder, were tempted, were slain with the sword: they wandered about in sheepskins and goatskins; being destitute, afflicted, tormented; (Of whom the world was not worthy:) they wandered in deserts, and in mountains, and in dens and caves of the earth. And these all, having obtained a good report through faith, received not the promise: God having provided some better thing for us, that they without us should not be made perfect.

It is my earnest prayer that this work will help to bring Bunyan back into the households of modern Christians, edify God's children through the life of this great saint of the past, and, above all else, glorify God.

Soli Deo Gloria

Jacob Tanner, 2022

CHAPTER 1

Humble Beginnings and Challenging Circumstances: The Early Life and Unlikely Origin of the Tinker

Christian: Now then, to prevent drowsiness in this place, let us fall into good discourse.

Hopeful: With all my heart.

Christian: Where shall we begin?

Hopeful: Where God began with us.

(*The Pilgrim's Progress*, Christian speaking with Hopeful on the enchanted ground)

You've likely seen the portrait: Holding a button bound book in his right hand, an ornate button robe around his torso, the Tinker looks at his painter, an ever-so-slight smile concealed beneath his curled mustache. His hair flows, his eyebrows are perhaps a bit too bushy, but one is almost immediately drawn to his eyes, which have a rare twinkle about them, peculiar to those who have found everlasting joy and happiness through Christ in this life. This is the portrait of John Bunyan, and subverts the expectations of what many expect to see when they hear the word 'Puritan.'

H.L. Mencken once famously quipped that Puritanism was, 'The haunting fear that someone, somewhere, may be happy.' Not only does Bunyan's portrait prove that the image of dour-faced, stiff-lipped, dull Puritans is farcical nonsense, but it also proves that the Tinker's writings are the greatest and most valuable insight into who he—and the other Puritans—actually were. Far removed from the image of Statler and Waldorf from *The Muppets* heckling whoever they could from the balcony box to disturb their fun, the Puritans were typically the ones being heckled by others because of their unwavering faith and deep joy in the Lord.

Yet, in many respects, Bunyan was not the typical Puritan, either. A Baptist at heart, he was startlingly uneducated when compared with most of his contemporaries. Yet, like other Puritans, he was a dissenter who eschewed the Church of England's mandate of conformity to the licensure process. Knowing the Lord had called him to preach, he would preach even if it meant years in prison. This serious devotion to Christ and his calling to preach makes a study of Bunyan's life increasingly valuable in an age of persecution, alongside his dissenting beliefs. But one must be careful when studying this almost larger-than-life figure to not lose sight of the portrait of the man—both the physical portrait and the one painted by his own writings. Rather than allowing the thoughts, ideas, and opinions of others to poison the portrait of who the man really was, we must look to him with honest eyes of discernment.

So, who exactly was this Tinker turned pastor—prisoner turned popular author and preacher? Who exactly was the man behind the portrait?

A Summarizing Glance

John Bunyan was born November 28, 1628, in Elstow, England, was baptized two days later on November 30, 1628, in a local parish of the Church of England, baptized by immersion in 1655 by Pastor John Gifford, and entered into glory and the tender embrace of his loving Savior on August 31, 1688. Only ten years prior to his passing, he published his most famous work: *The Pilgrim's Progress*, in 1678.

The son of a humble tinker (basically akin to the village blacksmith, who would travel to fix pots and pans), Bunyan spent nearly the first twenty-seven years of his life lost and in deep sin. His education was a meager affair, and he soon began assisting his father in the family trade before joining Cromwell's New Model Army at age sixteen. This was the young Tinker's first taste of Puritanism, and it would not be his last.

He was gloriously converted by God's grace, subsequently baptized in 1653 (though no record of this event now remains), and would begin preaching in 1655.[1] Bunyan would then spend a total of about twelve and a half of his brief fifty-nine years on earth imprisoned, after the restoration of the monarchy, for preaching without a license.

To put his life into perspective, this means that out of his thirty-three years as a Christian, only a little over twenty years were spent truly free. Yet, despite (or, perhaps, because of) his imprisonment, Bunyan left an amazing legacy of written classics. He published about 60 written works, including books and tracts.

His years of imprisonment did not stop him from preaching, either. He was the pastor of the church of the Bedford Meeting in the village of Elstow, part of Bedfordshire county. When he was eventually incarcerated for preaching, many of his congregation were imprisoned alongside him. Amazingly, like Paul during his imprisonments, Bunyan stayed active as a shepherd to the people and continued to minister to them in various ways. These prison stays were also the occasions where he was able to complete what is arguably some of his most important writings.

From sinner, to soldier, to Tinker, to saint, to preacher, to writer, Bunyan lived an extraordinary life. His writing and preaching are characteristic of rich, deep, warm, joyful, tender, loving, and experiential Puritan theology. Who could read the Tinker's writing and think him to be anything other than a loving and joyful child of God?

But every story has a beginning, and the Tinker's story, much like Christian's in *The Pilgrim's Progress*, has a surprisingly

---

1. See: George Offor, *Memoir of John Bunyan, The Works of John Bunyan*, 1:xxvi.

unlikely start. No one, except God who ordains all things, could have possibly imagined that the birth and childhood of this man would lead to one of the greatest Christian thinkers, preachers, and writers of all time.

A Surprisingly Impious, Poor, and Uneducated Upbringing

One of the surprises in Bunyan's works is that he rarely, if ever, truly speaks of his parents. They are mentioned, of course, but he never divulges a great deal of information about them. We know, for example, that his father's name was Thomas Bunyan and his mother's name was Margaret Bently. We know his father was a tinker, and was poor, but evidently owned some land. We know that his parents had him baptized after his birth, but this may have been because of social pressure, or for posterity's sake, more than any legitimate conviction. With such seldom mentions of his parentage, it is unsurprising that he never alludes to their holiness or piety.

Perhaps one of the best insights into his parentage is found within his work, *Christian Behavior*, wherein he closes the section on the duty of the godly child to ungodly parents with the following prayer: 'The Lord, if it be his will, convert our poor parents, that they, with us, may be the children of God.'[2] The fact that Bunyan writes with a possessive noun, praying for the conversion of '*our* poor parents,' does lead one to conclude it to be likely that his parents were not themselves Christians; or, at the very least, that they did not regularly display the fruit of the Spirit.

With so little information regarding the character of Bunyan's parents, it is difficult to conclude what their actual spiritual condition was. It would be easy to state that they were of the vastly ungodly sort, and this is what poisoned the young Tinker to become so wicked in his younger years, but that is not necessarily the case.

For example, in the Tinker's autobiographical work, *Grace Abounding to the Chief of Sinners*, in giving 'a few words' to divulge 'a hint' of his own 'pedigree,'[3] he writes about how his poor parents sent him to school. Though they may not

---

2. *Works*, 2:564.

3. John Bunyan, *Grace Abounding to the Chief of Sinners*, *Works*, 1:6.

have possessed the godliest of character, they did care enough to make sure their child would learn how to read and write. Though the profession of tinker would have left the family without much in the way of funds, John was cared for by his parents.

Speaking of his household's poverty, he explains that, 'For my descent then, it was, as is well known by many, of a low and inconsiderable generation; my father's house being of that rank that is meanest and most despised of all the families in the land.'[4] While we know that his father was a tinker, much else appears to be lost to history. In the *Memoir of John Bunyan*, not even his grandfather's name was known at the time of its composition. In fact, the biographical note about his heritage states that, 'This poverty-stricken, ragged tinker was the son of a working mechanic at Elstow, near Bedford. So obscure was his origin that even the Christian name of his father is yet unknown.'[5]

Yet, though the father's name was evidently unknown to these writers, it was thought, even within the *Memoir*, that Bunyan's father may have been a Gypsy, for the profession of tinker was one in which wandering bands of Gypsies were often employed. And, after all, within *Grace Abounding*, Bunyan mentions that, for a time, he had hoped to have descended from the Israelites and even asked his father, 'Whether we were of the Israelites or no? for, finding in the Scripture that they were once the peculiar people of God, thought I, if I were one of this race, my soul must needs be happy.'[6] Many at this time connected tinkers to the Gypsies, and Gypsies, to some, a lost tribe of Israel. George Offor, editor of his *Works*, notes that, 'Asking his father this question, looks a little as if the family had been connected with the gipsy tribe.'[7] And, in Offor's own *Memoir of Bunyan*, he concludes much the same, stating that the question he posed to his father, 'Somewhat justifies the

---

4. Ibid.
5. George Offor, *Memoir of John Bunyan*, *Works*, 1:ii.
6. Bunyan, *Grace Abounding to the Chief of Sinners*, *Works*, 1:8.
7. Ibid.

conclusion that his father was a Gipsy tinker, that occupation being then followed by the Gipsy tribe.'[8]

Whether or not Bunyan was of Gypsy origin is still debatable, though there is certainly a great deal of circumstantial evidence to support the claim. While some, like the Rev. John Brown, pastor of Bunyan Church in Bedford, believed that the Bunyan surname proved his family was part of 'a broken-down branch of the English aristocracy,'[9] others, like James Simson in his short work *Was John Bunyan a Gypsy?* had concluded that when Bunyan had described himself as descending from 'the meanest and most despised of *all* the families in the land,' and was 'not of the Israelites,' that the right conclusion to draw was that the Bunyans were '*not Jews*, but tinkers, that is, Gipsies of more or less mixed blood; so that his having been a tinker was in itself amply sufficient to prove Bunyan to have been of the Gipsy race; while it illustrated and confirmed his admission about "his father's house" having been of the Gipsy tribe.'[10] While this is a possible conclusion to draw from Bunyan's search for a Jewish origin, it is difficult to ascertain whether it has any basis of truth or if Bunyan's question was simply that of an eager youth who was looking for some shred of dignity in what he and others had concluded was an ignoble heritage.

Simson is very helpful, however, in determining some of the history of Bunyan's surname. From his own research, he had discovered, with interest, 'the letter from "Thomas Bunyan, chief warder, Tower of London, and born in Roxburghshire..."' The origin which he gives of the name is apparently the correct one, viz.: that "the first Bunyan was an Italian mason, who came to Melrose, and was at the building of that famous abbey in the year 1136;" and that "the oldest gravestone in the graveyard around Melrose Abbey has on it the name of Bunyan."'[11] This would put the family around Melrose Abbey in the eleventh century, and would mean that John's own

---

8.   Offor, *Memoir of John Bunyan, Works,* 1:iii.

9.   James Simson, *Was John Bunyan a Gipsy?* (New York: James Miller, 1882), 9-10. Accessed through Project Gutenberg.

10.   Ibid.

11.   Ibid., 11.

ancestors had made their way to Elstow, one hundred and seventy-three miles south-east of the Abbey, and fifty miles north of London, before his birth. Simson was unrelenting in his insistence of Gypsy origin. He would go on to write, 'In my *Disquisition on the Gipsies*, published in 1865, I said:—"The name Bunyan would seem to be of foreign origin" (p. 519). It does not necessarily follow that the blood of the Italian mason flowed in John Bunyan's veins, except by it having in some way got mixed with and merged in that of the Gipsy race.'[12] As far as Simson was concerned, Bunyan's search for Jewish ancestry, and the fact that his father was a tinker, was the greatest proof that he was descended from the Gypsies. In Bunyan's day, it was not unusual to associate the Gypsies with the Jews, and parents would sometimes tell their children, 'We must have been among the Jews, for some of our ceremonies are like theirs.'[13]

Furthermore, though the evidence is purely circumstantial, with no true admission from Bunyan himself, Simson makes a compelling case that the language he used in his writings to describe himself and his family was all the evidence needed to conclude his ancestry:

> I presume that no one will question the assertions that Bunyan was a tinker, and that English 'tinkers' are simply Gipsies of more or less mixed blood. Put together these three ideas—his description of his 'father's house,' and their not being Jews, but tinkers, that is, Gipsies of mixed blood—and you have the evidence or proof that John Bunyan was of the Gipsy race. If people are hanged on circumstantial evidence, cannot the same kind of proof be used to explain the language which Bunyan used to remind the world who and what he was, at a time when it was death by law for being a Gipsy, and 'felony without benefit of clergy' for associating with them, and odious to the rest of the population? From all that we know of Bunyan, we could safely conclude that he was not the man to leave the world in doubt as to who and what he was. He even reminded it of what it knew well; but with his usual discretion he abstained from using a word that was banned by the law of the land and the more despotic decree of society, and concluded that

---

12. Ibid.
13. Ibid.

it perfectly understood what he meant, although there was no necessity, or even occasion, for him to do what he did.[14]

Now, it is true that in Christ 'there is neither Jew nor Gentile,' (Gal. 3:28), so the ethnicity of the Bunyans is of little importance when considering the Tinker's citizenship in the celestial city. But, if it is correct to say that Bunyan was of Gypsy origin (which I am convinced it is), then it makes his position in society all the lower, and his eventual rise to fame as a Christian pastor and writer all the more surprising. Of course, God loves to use the unexpected. Note that in the genealogical account of Jesus' lineage through Joseph in Matthew 1, Matthew purposefully includes the mention of five women—unheard of in Ancient Near Eastern genealogical records!—and of these five, at least three had linkage with the Gentiles. Even our Lord and Savior's birth is unexpected and counted ignoble by many. Born of a virgin girl, no room in the inn, He entered the world in a manger, surrounded by the beasts of the field. Yet, this child born in such a disgraceful way was, and is, the King of kings and Lord of lords.

Bunyan's birth and lineage is somewhat like this. Until relatively recently, with the release of John Brown's biography on Bunyan in the late 1800's, not much was known of his ancestors. It's still possible the tinkers were related to Gypsies. Whatever the case, the Lord, in His sovereign providence, used the Bunyan clan to raise up the Tinker.

As mentioned above, Bunyan does, momentarily at least, write favorably of how his parents *did* send him to get an education for a short time. In his own words, 'Notwithstanding the meanness and inconsiderableness of my parents, it pleased God to put it into their hearts to put me to school, to learn both to read and write; the which I also attained, according to the rate of other poor men's children.'[15]

That his parents sent him to school, even for a short time, is commendable. Yet, Bunyan confessed that this meager education was not one that he retained for very long: 'To my shame I confess, I did soon lose that little I learned, and that

---

14. Ibid., 12.
15. Bunyan, *Grace Abounding to the Chief of Sinners*, *Works*, 1:6.

even almost utterly, and that long before the Lord did work his gracious work of conversion upon my soul.'[16]

This is something that Bunyan highlights himself on more than one occasion, and something his adversaries often attempted to wield against him, as though his lack of a strong education was a double-edged sword that both he and his enemies used to cut his pride. In the preface to *The Doctrine of Law and Grace Unfolded*, Bunyan writes, 'Reader, if thou do find this book empty of fantastical expressions, and without light, vain, whimsical, scholar-like terms; thou must understand, it is because I never went to school to Aristotle or Plato, but was brought up at my father's house, in a very mean condition, among a company of poor countrymen.'[17] Yet, despite these apparent faults in his own education, Bunyan was resolute in continuing to preach and teach theological and doctrinal truths.

His lack of education was not his only point of self-deprecation, however. It appears that his lineage, and economic status, were two other sources of continued criticism, both from others and himself. Sensing this, his own pastor, John Burton, wrote in his endorsement of Bunyan's *Some Gospel Truths Opened*:

> Reader, in this book thou wilt not meet with high flown airy notions, which some delight in, counting them high mysteries, but the sound, plain, common, (and yet spiritual and mysterious) truths of the gospel, and if thou art a believer, thou must needs reckon them so, and the more, if thou hast not only the faith of them in thy heart, but art daily living in the spiritual sense and feeling of them, and of thy interest in them. Neither doth this treatise offer to thee doubtful controversial things, or matters of opinion, as some books chiefly do, which when insisted upon, the weightier things of the gospel have always done more hurt than good: But here thou hast things necessary to be believed, which thou canst not too much study. Therefore pray, that thou mayest receive this word which is according to the scriptures in faith and love, not as the word of man, but as the word of God, without respect of persons, and be not offended because Christ holds forth the glorious

---

16. Ibid.

17. Bunyan, *The Doctrine of Law and Grace Unfolded*, *Works*, 1:495.

treasure of the gospel to thee in a poor earthen vessel, by one who hath neither the greatness nor the wisdom of this world to commend him to thee.[18]

Bunyan's lowly status in society, coupled with his meager education, only served to highlight the great grace and wisdom of God that had been bestowed upon his life. There was nothing significant about his upbring, nor anything spectacular about his education, that should have made him an author of nearly sixty works, including *The Pilgrim's Progress*. In an age of gifted and learned scholars and theologians, there was nothing that made the Tinker stand out among his peers. Yet, the Apostle Paul's words in 1 Corinthians 1:26-29 were proved true, over and over again, by the fantastical life of the Tinker lived in service to the Triune God:

> For ye see your calling, brethren, how that not many wise men after the flesh, not many mighty, not many noble, are called: But God hath chosen the foolish things of the world to confound the wise; and God hath chosen the weak things of the world to confound the things which are mighty; And base things of the world, and things which are despised, hath God chosen, yea, and things which are not, to bring to nought things that are: That no flesh should glory in his presence.

Perhaps Bunyan seemed as foolish in his own day as many would account him in our own, but that did not stop the Lord from using the Tinker in a mighty way, unimaginable to those who are less spiritually inclined. In the advertisement by the editor to his *Scriptural Poems*, there is an included note that, when reading Bunyan's poems, 'Our surprise will be excited, not by little inaccuracies of style or departures from the rules of grammar, but at the talent of a poor mechanic, in so faithfully rendering scripture histories in such simple and striking language.'[19] That Bunyan's education was a meager affair is little to be doubted. In this same preface, the editor explains that, 'As Mr. Burton says, in commending his Gospel Truths Vindicated,—"This man hath not the learning or wisdom of man, yet through grace he hath received the

---

18. Bunyan, *Some Gospel Truths Opened*, Works, 2:140.
19. Offor, *Advertisement for Scriptural Poems*, Works, 2:386.

teaching of God, and the learning of the Spirit of Christ, which is the thing that makes a man both a Christian and a minister of the gospel. (Is. 50:4).'"[20] Not all were so kind to the Tinker though. It was with his own quarrel with those who were to be known as the *Strict Baptists*, wherein they argued over the position of open membership and open communion (which Bunyan supported), that the Tinker wrote to his challengers in the opening to *Differences in Judgment about Water Baptism, No Bar to Communion*, 'You closely disdain my person because of my low descent among men, stigmatizing me as a person of THAT rank that need not be heeded or attended unto.'[21] It would appear that, in the debate over open and closed communion, some had taken to attacking the rank of the Tinker, or his place in society, to discredit his positions. But the Tinker seems to have grown accustomed to such assaults against his birth and upbringing, so that he was readily able to defend himself against even the fiercest of attempts at character assassination. In this same work, the Tinker states:

> And why is MY rank so mean, that the most gracious and godly among you, may not duly and soberly consider of what I have said? Was it not the art of the false apostles of old to say thus? To bespatter a man, that his doctrine might be disregarded. 'Is not this the carpenter?' And, 'His bodily presence *is* weak and *his* speech contemptible,' (1 Co. X. 10), did not use to be in the mouths of the saints; for they knew that 'the wind bloweth where it listeth.' (Jn. iii. 8). Neither is it high birth, worldly breeding, or wealth; but electing love, grace, and the wisdom that comes from heaven, that those who strive for strictness of order in the things and kingdom of Christ, should have in regard and esteem. (Ja. iii. 17)... Why then do you despise my rank, my state, and quality in the world?[22]

Bunyan was right, of course. Those who are the true children of God know it to be of certain truth that God, to shame the apparently wise of the world, will often call the apparently

---

20. Ibid., 386.

21. Bunyan, *Differences in Judgment about Water Baptism, No Bar to Communion*, *Works*, 2:617.

22. Ibid., 618.

foolish. Other times, to shame the rich, the Lord will call the poor. In Bunyan's case, God shamed those of noble births and high education with His calling forth of the poor and unlearned Tinker.

Returning now to the subject of Bunyan's parents, we note that they were themselves likely poor, unlearned, and, perhaps, unsaved. Again, Bunyan had prayed within his *Christian Behaviour*, 'The Lord, if it be his will, convert our poor parents, that they, with us, may be the children of God.'[23] George Offor, in the footnotes of *Christian Behavior* notes of this prayer that:

> Bunyan's silence, in all his writings, concerning the state of his parents as to godliness, may lead us to fear that this fervent ejaculation had often been poured forth by his own soul on behalf of his father and mother. All that we know of them is, that they were poor, but gave their children the best education their means afforded; as to their piety he is silent.[24]

And, again, Offor writes in the footnotes of *Grace Abounding to the Chief of Sinners* that:

> Bunyan says very little about his parents in his treatise on 'Christian Behavior;' he concludes his observations on the duties of a pious son to ungodly parents with this remarkable prayer… Although this does not demonstrate that his own parents were ungodly, yet his silence as to their piety upon all occasions when speaking of them, and the fervent feeling expressed in this short prayer, inclines me to conclude that they were not pious persons in his judgment.[25]

Though they were, evidently, likely not Christians, or at least not pious Christians, it was the divine hand of Providence that had caused the young Tinker to be born into a village in which 'it was a disgrace to any parents not to have their children educated.'[26] Despite their poor economic status, there was a sort of charity that had been established for the poor children of Bedford to receive a small education. Documentation from

---

23. Bunyan, *Christian Behaviour, Works*, 2:564.
24. Offor, *Christian Behavior, Works*, 2.564.
25. Offor, *Grace Abounding to the Chief of Sinners, Works*, 1:6.
26. Offor, *Memoir of John Bunyan, Works*, 1:iii.

the time has shown that 'In 1566, Sir Thomas Harper, Lord Mayor of London, gave £180 for thirteen acres and a rood of meadow land in Holborn. This was settled, in trust, to promote the education of the poor in and round Bedford. In 1668, it produced a yearly revenue of £99—a considerable sum in that day...'[27] It may not have been much, it may not have lasted very long, and Bunyan may have claimed to have soon forgotten it, but this education would prove to be quite important in his later years as he set about writing some of the most valuable works to ever depart from the pen of a Christian.

It is, frankly, amusing to read in Bunyan's *Scriptural Poems*, a stanza wherein he states:

> I am no poet, nor a poet's son
> But a mechanic, guided by no rule
> But what I gained in a grammar school,
> In my minority.[28]

Perhaps he was not a *learned* poet, but he had the heart of one.[29] His poetry, allegory, and general writings always have a winsome and delightful quality about them. But like most poets worth reading, Bunyan learned to write in a way that glorified God after first suffering through a great deal many sins and godly conviction over those sins.

A Childhood of Besetting Sins and a Nearly Seared Conscience

It is unsurprising that an evident lack of godly and pious parentage led Bunyan into the deep chasm of devilish delights and childish wickedness. Like most children left to their own devices, Bunyan was notoriously active in his pursuit of evil and wickedness. His was not so much a situation of the devil

---

27. Ibid.

28. Bunyan, *Scriptural Poems, Works*, 2:390.

29. Though his lack of education meant that he never actually studied some of the great and classic poets, he at least had some familiarity with the inestimable George Herbert and his magnum opus *The Temple*, and quotes from it:
'If what the learned Herbert says, holds true
A verse may find him, who a sermon flies,
And turn delight into a sacrifice.' (See: *Scriptural Poems, Works*, 2:390).

finding work for idle hands to do, so much as it was a young sinner pursuing iniquity with brazen speed and without delay. In his own words, 'It was my delight to be "taken captive by the devil at his will." 2 Ti. ii. 26.'[30]

Like David spotting Bathsheba bathing on the rooftop, and then delighting in his adulterous affair without repentance for some time, the young Tinker was truly pleased with his great deal of sinning. There was little respite when it came to his pursual of evil. If one would have seen him sinning as a child, they may have been forgiven for doubting that the Lord would ever use such a child in such a glorious way. But, where sin abounds, grace abounds all the more! (Rom. 5:20).

As a child, Bunyan admitted that, 'I had but few equals, especially considering my years, which were tender, being few, both for cursing, swearing, lying, and blaspheming the holy name of God.'[31] This was no ordinary sinning; this was the sinning of one 'Being filled with all unrighteousness, fornication, wickedness, covetousness, maliciousness; full of envy, murder, debate, deceit, malignity; whisperers, Backbiters, haters of God, despiteful, proud, boasters, inventors of evil things, disobedient to parents, Without understanding, covenantbreakers, without natural affection, implacable, unmerciful: Who knowing the judgment of God, that they which commit such things are worthy of death, not only do the same, but have pleasure in them that do them.' (Rom. 1:29-32). It is nothing short of a miracle that the Tinker was never turned over to a reprobate and seared conscience that would refuse to repent and believe. It was nothing less than the electing love and grace of the Triune God that rescued Bunyan from eternal damnation.

While still a child, and while engaged in a plethora of wicked sins, the Tinker began to have terrible dreams. These dreams, actually nightmares, were a grace sent from the Lord because they continually warned the child of evil spirits, demons, the coming judgment, and the wrath of God. These dreams did not convert the young Tinker (only the proclamation of the gospel, coupled with the indwelling and regenerating work of

---

30. Bunyan, *Grace Abounding to the Chief of Sinners, Works*, 1:6.
31. Ibid.

the Holy Spirit can accomplish that), but they did restrain the boy from gleefully continuing in his sin without consideration for the estate of his own soul. Of these childhood dreams and nightmares, he records that:

> I also have with soberness considered since, did so offend the Lord, that even in my childhood he did scare and affright me with fearful dreams, and did terrify me with dreadful visions; for often, after I had spent this and the other day in sin, I have in my bed been greatly afflicted, while asleep, with the apprehensions of devils and wicked spirits, who still, as I then thought, laboured to draw me away with them, of which I could never be rid.[32]

While such dreaming may seem strange within a modern western context, such superstitious spirituality was not out of place in Bedford during the early and mid-seventeenth century. Consider that the famous Salem Witch Trials took place at the end of the seventeenth century, and that many who settled the new world came from villages not unlike Bunyan's own Bedford, and it is easy to see that it was a time wherein people were more prone to seeing the supernatural, even where it didn't necessarily exist, than modern people are today.

Take, for example, the writings of Martin Luther, whose own writings had a great deal of influence over the Tinker after his conversion to Christianity. In the sixteenth century, the Magisterial Reformer wrote often about Satan and his attacks. While some may simply dismiss this as a case of pre-enlightenment leftovers of middle age superstitions, Luther and the other Reformers would likely have thought such a view crazy—they truly believed the devil existed and could exert a great deal of power. For example, there is a famous anecdotal story of how, one day, Luther felt oppressed by Satan and so, in a fit of anger, threw his ink well at the devil. Some state that even today, if one was to look at the wall of Luther's home, they would find the spot where Luther struck the devil with ink. While it is unlikely the story actually happened as described, it also is not difficult to imagine that Luther may

---

32. *Works*, 1:6.

have, at one point, thrown his ink well at the wall because he *thought* Satan was there.

Once, however, Luther did write, 'Apart from the forgiveness of sins I can't stand a bad conscience at all; the devil hounds me about a single sin until the world becomes too small for me … while God loves life, the devil hates life.'[33] It was not unusual, then, for many Reformers, and then their Puritan descendants, to deduce the presence of Satan and demonic influences in their day-to-day lives.

For Bunyan, living as a young child in Bedford in the seventeenth century, he likely had many occasions to hear talk of devils, demons, and even hell. However, without godly parents to truly encourage him to seek the Lord Jesus Christ for forgiveness of sins and victory over Satan, he had only the notion that Satan was powerful, and he was weak. He could only see hell as the destination toward which he was constantly heading, with no means of escape and no Savior in sight to rescue him from his soul's plunge into despair. 'At these years,' he wrote that he was, 'greatly afflicted and troubled with the thoughts of the day of judgment, and that both night and day, and should tremble at the thoughts of the fearful torments of hell fire; still fearing that it would be my lot to be found at last amongst those devils and hellish fiends, who are there bound down with the chains and bonds of eternal darkness, "unto the judgment of the last day."'[34] All the same, as we will see in later chapters, these thoughts and nightmares of hell did have their own peculiar role to play in leading Bunyan to Christ.

There is, once more, a great deal of similarity with Martin Luther's own experience of conviction of sin. After Luther had completed and earned his Master's degree, he was on his way back to Erfurt, where he would begin his studies as a law student. On the way, he was caught in a terrible storm and, when lightning struck near where he was, he was thrown from his horse to the ground below. It was in that moment

---

33. Martin Luther, *Luther's Works*, ed. and trans. Theodore G. Tappert, vol. 54, *Table Talk* (Philadelphia: Fortress Press, 1967), 34.

34. Bunyan, *Grace Abounding to the Chief of Sinners*, *Works*, 1:6.

that he swore an oath to St Anne that, if she would help him, he would become a monk.

Both Luther and Bunyan had a poor theological understanding of who God was at this point, but they were aware of a coming judgment. They wrestled with sin and devils and hell, but did not know from whence their help would, or even could, come. Thus, they did what they had been taught by others to do. In Luther's case, his Roman Catholic upbringing led him to cry out to a supposed saint and make a rash vow to try and save his own life. In Bunyan's case, the frightening nightmares led him to often feel cast down and dejected, even amongst his peers, but because he lacked the religious background that Luther had, the young Tinker could only look to his peers for advice. Thus, despite a conviction of sin and fear of coming judgment, he gave himself over to even greater sin.

This is not to say that the tormenting thoughts and dreams of devils and demons would leave him unaffected. On the contrary, this torment would lead him to write, 'Yea, I was "also then" so overcome with despair of life and heaven, that I should often wish either that there had been no hell, or that I had been a devil—supposing they were only tormentors; that if it must needs be that I went thither, I might be rather a tormentor than "be" tormented myself.'[35]

But the dreams failed to keep him from pursuing his youthful lusts and sinful passions. 'For my pleasures,' he wrote, 'did quickly cut off the remembrance of them, as if they had never been: wherefore, with more greediness, according to the strength of nature, I did still let loose the reins to my lusts, and delighted on all transgression against the law of God.'[36] Not only did the dreams apparently harden him in his sins, but, until his first marriage, he became 'the very ringleader of all the youth that kept me company, into all manner of vice and ungodliness.'[37]

Bunyan recognized, later in life, that even in his fanatical pursuit of sin, the grace of God was working to restrain and

35. Ibid.
36. Ibid.
37. Ibid., 6-7.

constrain him from being as sinful as he could possibly be. Had it not been from this dispensation of common grace upon the Tinker, then he surely would have perished eternally in hell. But the Lord had great plans for this most ignoble of young men, and those plans would be brought to fulfillment.

Unfortunately, Bunyan's conversion was still a few years away and his most wretched and deplorable condition would only exacerbate until that time that the Father had appointed for him to be saved would come to pass.

CHAPTER 2

Debauched Living: The Profane and Vain Promiscuity of Bunyan Before Conversion and the Nature of His Day

So he went on, and Apollyon met him. Now the monster was hideous to behold: he was clothed with scales, like a fish (and they are his pride), he had wings like a dragon, and feet like a bear, and out of his belly came fire and smoke, and his mouth was as the mouth of a lion. When he was come up to Christian, he beheld him with a disdainful countenance, and thus began to question him.

Apollyon: Whence came you? and whither are you bound?

Christian: I am come from the city of Destruction, which is the place of all evil, and am going to the city of Zion.

Apollyon: By this I perceive thou art one of my subjects, for all that country is mine, and I am the prince and god of it. How is it, then, that thou hast run away from thy king? Were it not that I hope thou mayest do me more service, I would strike thee now, at one blow, to the ground.

Christian: I was born, indeed, in your dominions, but your service was hard, and your wages such as a man could not live on, 'for the wages of sin *is* death,' Ro. vi.23; therefore,

when I was come to years, I did as other considerate persons
do, look out, if, perhaps, I might mend myself.

Apollyon: There is no prince that will thus lightly lose
his subjects, neither will I as yet lose thee; but since thou
complainest of thy service and wages, be content to go back;
what our country will afford, I do here promise to give thee.

Christian: But I have let myself to another, even to the King
of princes; and how can I with fairness go back with thee?

(Christian, battling Apollyon, *The Pilgrim's Progress*)

It should hardly come as a surprise that a child, already
living wretchedly, and without godly parents to redirect
his course in life, would continue to fall into all manner of
debauchery. Bunyan's early life proved the Proverb true: 'As
a dog returneth to his vomit, so a fool returneth to his folly'
(Prov. 26:11). Except, each time he returned to his folly and
sins, it was as though the sinning only increased and grew
all the worse. Day by day, the young man became more and
more like a wretched demon than a man created in the image
of God. He was living in such a dreadful state of iniquity that,
one may say, the chains of sin that had enslaved him were
also drawing him closer and closer to the flaming pit of hell,
day by day.

One cannot help but wonder where the young Tinker's
parents were in his childhood. One may wonder further
whether there was any sort of godly influence, or correction,
that he received in these early years at all. Proverbs 29:15
warns that, 'The rod and reproof give wisdom: but a child
left to himself bringeth his mother to shame.' The poor wretch
was apparently left to his own devices, and regularly brought
shame upon himself, his family, and his friends.

The danger of looking at Bunyan's sinful youth is twofold:
His sin may be glorified, or, perhaps worse still, one may look
down on the child and think themselves more holy than he.
Let it be noted here that Bunyan's sinful youth is not to be
celebrated, but it is to be instructive: Should one be reading

this who is still in sin, then flee from your sin and run to the embrace of Christ! He alone can save.

If there be one reading this who is raising children, then let this examination of the young Tinker encourage you to fulfill your duty in raising your children in the nurture and admonition of the Lord. God used Bunyan in spite of his great many sins, but imagine how much greater the Tinker may have been if he had never fallen into such serious and heinous sins in his childhood. Imagine what may have been if he had had godly parents correcting, disciplining, and pointing him to Christ.

While it is remarkably sad that the young John did not have godly parents to lead him, his young life of corruption does also serve to prove the reality of total depravity in the heart of all men, from the moment of birth. John Calvin once noted in his *Institutes* that, 'When viewing our miserable condition since Adam's fall, all confidence and boasting are overthrown, we blush for shame, and feel truly humble... It is impossible to think of our primeval dignity without being immediately reminded of the sad spectacle of our ignominy and corruption, ever since we fell from our original in the person of our first parent.'[1]

The doctrine of total depravity is often misunderstood by many in this world, including some Christians, but is clearly witnessed in the young Tinker. Children, even at young and tender ages, betray their youthful exteriors and brandish their iniquitous natures continually through their actions. As some have observed, none need teach a child how to sin—the sinning comes naturally. What a child needs is direction in piety, holiness, and righteousness; that is to say, a child needs to be pointed toward Jesus and the hope that is found in His gospel alone.

It would be years, still, before John would encounter the gospel and, through the drawing power of the Holy Spirit, be compelled to come to Jesus. Thus, we now begin an earnest look at his childhood and what the experience may have been like.

---

1. John Calvin, *Institutes of the Christian Religion*, trans. Henry Beveridge (Peabody, MA: Hendrickson Publishers, 2008), II.I.I.

Ringleader of the Tormentors

First Corinthians 15:33 commands us to, 'Be not deceived: evil communications corrupt good manners.' That is to say, bad company will corrupt the good. One bad apple can make the whole batch rotten. But, what of bad company with bad morals keeping even worse company? That was the plight of Bunyan's youth. He was a wicked son who surrounded himself with wicked company, yet he was more wicked than they. He was, by his own admission, '[T]he very ringleader of all the youth that kept me company, into all manner of vice and ungodliness.'[2]

Imagine, as a child, being left to your own devices, to do as you pleased, with a group of friends as wicked as you, without anyone ever stepping in to challenge your actions or teach you about the Lord's everlasting and enduring punishments against sin. It is likely that some need not imagine such a childhood because it is familiar to you already. Others may be very unfamiliar with such a concept indeed, having been blessed with Christ-like examples in godly parents and guardians. Bunyan was, evidently, of the former group, and it appears likely that many of his friends that he led into sin were also lacking the example of Christian morality in the adult supervision surrounding them.

It is difficult to say where the young boy's parents were when he was raising mischief. What has been recorded about them leads one to believe that they cared little for their boy's morality or holiness. Indeed, 'Bunyan's parents do not appear to have checked, or attempted to counteract, his unbridled career of wickedness.'[3] Complicating the matter of his supervision further is the story of how, once, after being rebuked for his cursing, the young Tinker fell into a depressed state of worldly sorrow and wrote:

> At this reproof I was silenced, and put to secret shame; and
> that too, as I thought, before the God of heaven; wherefore,
> while I stood there, and hanging down my head, I wished with
> all my heart that I might be a little child again, that my father

2. John Bunyan, *Grace Abounding to the Chief of Sinners*, *Works*, 1:6-7.

3. George Offor, *Memoir of John Bunyan*, *Works*, 1:iii.

might learn me to speak without this wicked way of swearing; for, thought I, I am so accustomed to it, that it is in vain for me to think of a reformation; for I thought it could never be.[4]

This is a sad, almost chilling plea from a young man. He longed for a father who would have taught him the ways of righteous action and holy speech. He wished his father had taught him the secret of not allowing 'corrupt communication' to proceed from his mouth, but his father had not taught him to speak only that 'which is good to the use of edifying, that it may minister grace unto the hearers' (Eph. 4:29). It may be that his father had done the opposite of what he wished; perhaps Bunyan had learned how to curse and swear from his parents. It is no secret that children will often mimic their parents. After all, the Apostle Paul commands Christians, 'Be ye therefore followers of God, *as dear children...*' (Eph. 5:1, emphasis mine) because children follow in the footsteps of their parents. We are to follow God as children follow their parents; we are to be imitators of God as children imitate parents. Young John's speech must have been learned, and imitated, from somewhere: Is it not possible that he had grown accustomed to hearing his own parents speak in such a vile manner?

Whatever the case, without any sort of godly influence or supervision from the adults around him, he was left to continue in his own sins, and to lead others to follow him in this distressing lifestyle. He claims to have been the chief of sinners and provides a list of some of his most heinous crimes against the Lord, stating, 'From a child... I had but few equals (especially considering my years, which were tender, being but few) both for cursing, swearing, lying, and blaspheming the holy name of God.'[5]

It is interesting to note that each of these sins relates to the tongue. James 3:2 states that, 'If any man offend not in word, the same is a perfect man, and able also to bridle the whole body.' Considering that Bunyan *did* offend in word, and had not the ability to bridle his tongue, he would have lacked all power to bridle his body. The one who curses, swears, lies,

---

4. Bunyan, *Grace Abounding to the Chief of Sinners*, *Works*, 1:9.
5. Ibid., 6.

and blasphemes likely breaks every other commandment regularly as well for the tongue reveals the nature of a man. Indeed, his speech gives us the clearest insight into the state of his heart, for 'A good man out of the good treasure of his heart bringeth forth that which is good; and an evil man out of the evil treasure of his heart bringeth forth that which is evil: for of the abundance of the heart his mouth speaketh' (Luke 6:45). Yet, let it not be lost on us that this young man who regularly cursed, swore, lied, and blasphemed would eventually be used by God to become one whose tongue and pen would utter and write the most beautiful and glorious of truths.

As for his sins against the Lord, he also claimed to have most delighted in sinning on the Sabbath. After hearing a sermon that spoke of the evils of breaking the Sabbath, he claimed, 'Now, I was, notwithstanding my religion, one that took much delight in all manner of vice, and especially that was the day that I did solace myself therewith.'[6] It seems that Bunyan meant that he both neglected to rest on the Sabbath and to keep the Sabbath day holy, and he delighted most in sinning on God's holy day.

Much else of his childhood is lost. Thus, to learn about who he really was as a child, we will now look at what life was like for the youth of the mid-seventeenth century.

Growing Up in the Mid-seventeenth Century

Bunyan does not record a great deal of information regarding his childhood. He hardly wrote of his early years. This makes a direct examination of his young life rather difficult. However, when examining the information that he has provided, it is a great deal of help to also examine what life would have been like for a child growing up in the mid-seventeenth century in England.

In the twenty-first century, for most major parts of the world, it is almost unimaginable that children would be allowed to roam about without adult supervision and protection. However, only thirty years ago, it was not abnormal to see scores of children outside of their homes and playing on the

---

6. Ibid., 8.

streets, with hardly an adult in sight. Nearly four hundred years ago, things were far different still. In an age with no means of instant communication, the idea of 'helicopter parenting' was as foreign in parts of England as the New World was in distance.

Bunyan was, likely, allowed to scurry off into the town square and outskirts of town without so much as a 'be careful.' It was a different age, yes, but children were also expected to take on greater responsibilities at much younger ages. It would not have been out of the question for children, perhaps seven or eight years of age, to begin work as apprentices.

This was also an incredibly turbulent period in time. A century before, the Protestant Reformation had lit Europe on fire and shaped much of Bunyan's own day. Some of these events in the century leading up to his birth are essential to understand.

The Roman Catholic Church had lost its monolithic grip on Western Europe. The English Reformation, spearheaded by men like Thomas Cranmer, Hugh Latimer, and Nicholas Ridley, had swept across the land in the sixteenth century. King Henry VIII had broken away from the Roman Catholic Church in 1534 to establish the Church of England, but his desire for doing so was less than honorable: Pope Clement VII had refused to allow Henry to divorce his wife, and so the king decided the best thing to do was start a church of his own that would permit him to divorce his wife.

The Church of England was not as major of a reform movement as that of the Lutheran and Calvinist movements. While it did break away from the rule and reign of the Roman Papacy, King Henry VIII was not overly concerned with reforming the practices of the church and appeared to be content with many of the Roman Catholic practices he had grown accustomed to. But, under his son, King Edward VI, there would be a great reformation within the Church of England, and in 1549, and later 1552, Thomas Cranmer's *Book of Common Prayer* was instituted to lead the liturgy of the Church of England. There was even a confession written during this time, *The Forty-Two Articles*, later rewritten and remembered today as the *Thirty-Nine Articles*.

Then, a very dark time came when Queen 'Bloody' Mary became ruler after Edward VI. The Protestant persecution began once more in earnest, and the Roman Catholic Mary earned her 'Bloody' moniker when she had around three hundred English Reformers martyred.

When Mary died without child during an influenza epidemic—possibly from cancer—her half-sister, Elizabeth I, became Queen. Her rule fared better for the Protestants than Mary's did, but the Reformation suffered. Elizabeth did not persecute the Protestants as her sister did, but instead sought a middle ground between the teachings of the Reformation and Roman Catholicism regarding ecclesial authority. Some worried that the goal was to marry together Protestant convictions with Roman Catholic traditions. The result was a strange amalgamation of Protestant doctrines with a smattering of the old Roman Catholic traditions. This led directly to the rise of the Puritans, who felt strongly that the Reformation was not over. Though fairly young, the Puritans believed the Church of England needed to be reformed and purified from all ties to Roman Catholicism. It was, effectively, only 'half reformed.' Not least of the issues would eventually center around the *Book of Common Prayer* in the 1660s and would lead to the Great Ejection of the Puritans in 1662.

Only a few decades prior to John's birth, England had experienced a golden age of sorts, under the reign of Elizabeth I. Now, in the mid-seventeenth century, Protestants were fighting against Protestants, as Puritans arose against those within the Church of England, noting the need for a Reformation within the Church of England, which some worried had quickly become as corrupt an institution as the Roman Catholic Church was when Martin Luther had stood against it.

Because of the religious turmoil, there was also a great deal of war and armed combat taking place during the majority of Bunyan's life. Consider the English Civil War, a series of civil wars between the Parliamentarians and Royalists, that were fought between 1642 and 1651. The young Tinker would have been about fourteen at the start of the war and would even join Cromwell's New Model Army at one point. His life was spared by the divine hand of Providence when a fellow soldier, taking his place, was killed with a musket.

The ruler that Bunyan would have been familiar with as a child and then soldier was King Charles I. He was ruler of England from 1625 to 1649, and at the end of the English Civil War, would become the only English monarch to be executed for treason. His reign was almost always tumultuous at best, and the English Civil War was evidence of this. It can be a great effort to follow the various sides in their fighting, figuring out who is on what side and at what point. In her biography of Charles, *The White King*, Leanda de Lisle wrote of the English Civil War:

> In fact this is to be a war of Protestant against Protestant over the nature of the Church of England, and where exactly the balance of power between king and Parliament lies. Many MPs will fight for the king's cause. And many MPs who begin by fighting against him, end up fighting against their former comrades...[7]

Around this same time, William Laud had become bishop of England. He would later become archbishop of Canterbury. Joel Beeke and Paul Smalley wrote that, during this time, under the rule of Charles I and Bishop Laud, 'Those holding to Reformed doctrine and piety found themselves in ever-increasing disfavor in church and state as a result of the rise of Laud's high-church Arminian party.'[8] Considering Bunyan's baptism into the Church of England when he was a few days old, this is the doctrine and polity he would have been most familiar with as a child.[9]

The young Bunyan would not have had a great deal of serious Reformed preaching or teaching around him as a boy, either. Some of the Puritans, displeased and unsatisfied with the state of affairs in which they found themselves, began to leave for the new world in 1620, before Bunyan's birth,

7.   Leanda de Lisle, *The White King: Charles I, Traitor, Murderer, Martyr* (New York: Hachette Book Group, 2017), xxii. Kindle Edition.

8.   Joel R. Beeke and Paul M. Smalley, *John Bunyan and the Grace of Fearing God* (Philipsburg: P&R Publishing, 2016), 2.

9.   See: Vera Brittain, *In the Steps of John Bunyan: An Excursion into Puritan England* (London, UK: Rich and Cowan, 1950), 44.

and in 1630, a Puritan exodus was led to the new world by John Winthrop.[10] Only a few decades prior, the Tinker would have had no shortage of Puritans to learn from. By the date of his birth in 1628, the number of Puritans had significantly decreased, and by the time he was two years old, an even greater number would depart from the land. It is almost impossible to say how different his childhood may have been if there had been a larger number of Puritans still in the land.

Perhaps all this conflict, treason, and war made the parents of the children in Elstow uneasy. While there is no way to tell how much these events impacted the Bunyan clan, being as far removed from London as they were, it would not be long until John was swept up into the swirling chaos himself when he joined the war effort on Cromwell's side. Those still holding to Puritan sensibilities, who had not voyaged to the New World, must have known that their numbers were dwindling in an increasingly hostile land. The children, then, would have heard talk of these things and the hushed murmurs of their parents, questioning the state of affairs in London, wondering about the true freedom of religion, and the reliability of monarchs. Rather unwittingly, the parents in Elstow may have planted the seeds of nonconformity into their children.

Considering the turmoil of the age, and the common talk in Elstow which likely centered around these many issues and problems, it is little surprise that Bunyan was also preoccupied often with thoughts of hell, demons, and Satan. A child surrounded by constant war, uncertainty, and bloodshed will necessarily think of such things. Without any true religious teaching to guide him, his thoughts took on a more supernatural bend. He wrote of how, during his childhood, 'Also I should, at these years, be greatly afflicted and troubled with the thoughts of the fearful torments of hell-fire; still fearing, that it would be my lot to be found at last among those devils and hellish fiends, who are there bound down with the chains and bonds of darkness, unto the judgment of the great day.'[11]

---

10. Ibid.
11. Bunyan, *Grace Abounding to the Chief of Sinners*, *Works*, 1:6.

Yes, the young Tinker thought about death and the afterlife often, but he sadly would have known next to nothing regarding the true state of the afterlife. Without proper biblical teaching and catechesis taking place—or, at least, without his paying attention to such teaching—his thoughts of the afterlife were heavily influenced by the superstitions surrounding him and rampant imagination within him. Yet, the fact that he knew something of an afterlife at all is due solely to the sovereign grace of Almighty God. These thoughts would be a sobering reality, counteracting a great deal of sin he would have otherwise committed and engaged in.

Though his parents were not as pious as one may wish, they likely knew something of religion and shared that with the young child. It is also likely that, since they had him baptized at two days old, they would have also brought him to church on the Sabbath. Just as today, there were those in Bunyan's day who participated in what may be called a nominal Christianity; that is to say, there were those who held to no true faith in the Lord Jesus Christ, but attended Sunday services simply because it was the thing to do and social standing depended on it. But even if he or his parents went for all the wrong reasons and hardly paid attention, only spending the time in the scheming of more mischief, it would have been hard to escape the lessons about eternal life, Christ as Savior, sin, death, and hell. Like listening to a new language while sleeping, the truth of God's Word has a way of infiltrating the heart and conscious of even the most hardened of sinners.

This confrontation with the Word of God, as small as it may have been, was important for the child because Bunyan regularly encountered death around him. In fact, one may conclude that the simple reason the young Tinker was so preoccupied with death was because he was, quite literally, often surrounded by it. Besides wars and common sicknesses, accidents and injuries were common during this age. Lynda Payne writes:

> Boys, unless they were from the noblest of families, were expected to serve an apprenticeship. They were often placed in dangerous crafts such as tanning, blacksmithing, or serving on

ships, where chemical poisonings, fires, and war injuries were frequent occurrences. There are also accounts in diaries of the period of youthful pranks leading to injury, for example, hiding gunpowder in candles so they blew up when lit.[12]

This was a highly tumultuous and combustible age of wars and rumors of wars. But the day-to-day trials of living in the mid-seventeenth century continued to exist as well. It is solely by God's grace that the Tinker saw adulthood and conversion.

Can God Really Use a Wretch like Thee?

While it is unfortunate that Bunyan regularly committed such terrible and heinous sins and blasphemies against the Lord, it was this experience with a plethora of sins, and an acknowledgement of his own wickedness, that would ultimately lead to his deep contrition and fervent seeking of Christ after conversion. Romans 8:28 promises that, 'And we know that all things work together for good to them that love God, to them who are the called according to his purpose.' Bunyan's early life of sin is proof of this. What would have amounted to a pitiful life of debauchery was transformed into a life of piety by the Lord who has said that He, 'Declar[es] the end from the beginning, and from ancient times the things that are not yet done, saying, My counsel shall stand, and I will do all my pleasure...' (Isa. 46:10). The God who, 'calleth those things which be not as though they were,' (Rom. 4:17) was able to use the many sins of Bunyan's youth to prepare him for a later call to gospel ministry, wherein he would be able to utilize his own experiences to preach to sinners worse than he.

Furthermore, it is amazing to see the divine and providential hand of the Lord directing the course of history in such a way that Bunyan was born at the perfect time and place to become the well-known Puritan he would become. If it were not for the English Reformation, the establishment of the Church of England, decades of persecution, and the rise of Puritanism, it is possible that Bunyan would never have been

12. Lynda Payne, 'Health in England (16th–18th c.),' in Children and Youth in History, Item #166, https://chnm.gmu.edu/cyh/teaching-modules/166.html (accessed December 2, 2021).

led into war, later experienced conversion, been arrested for nonconformity, and then written *The Pilgrim's Progress* or the plethora of other Christian classics he penned that the Lord has used to bless the world. Like reading the genealogical record of Christ's birth in Matthew 1 or Luke 3, studying the events that led up to and surrounded Bunyan's life reveals how God continually uses events and moments throughout history that seem terribly irredeemable to accomplish His greatest glory and the greatest good of His saints. Praise the Lord that He can even use sin in a non-sinful way.

Even the early years of Bunyan's sin were able to be redeemed by the Lord and utilized in such a way that the Tinker would reach an even greater number of lost souls with gospel truths. Reading the Apostle Paul's writings, the Christian cannot help but be struck by Paul's astonishment of God's grace. He believed himself to be the least of the Apostles (1 Cor. 15:9), the least of all the saints (Eph. 3:8), and the chief of sinners (1 Tim. 1:15), yet could honestly claim that he was saved 'by grace... through faith; and that not of [myself]: it is the gift of God. Not of works, lest any man should boast' (Eph. 2:8-9). Thinking on the miracle of salvation, Paul could only conclude, 'O the depth of the riches both of the wisdom and knowledge of God! how unsearchable are his judgments, and his ways past finding out!' (Rom. 11:33).

Reading Bunyan's writing provides one with very similar insight. The reason why the Tinker's sermons and writings were, and continue to be, so piercing, 'even to the dividing asunder of soul and spirit, and of the joints and marrow,' and able to be a 'discerner of the thoughts and intents of the heart' (Heb. 4:12), is because he knew the amazement of saving grace in his own life and had come to love the God who saved him, and especially His Word.[13]

This deep and lasting knowledge of the grace of God toward a poor sinner is evidenced again and again by the Tinker's

---

13. This is not to suggest that Bunyan's sermons or other writings are inspired, inerrant, or infallible like Scripture is. Bunyan's writings are the words of a man, whereas the Bible is the Word of God. This is to say that his writings have the peculiar quality of one who has been deeply touched and affected by the grace of God as revealed through His Word.

writings. Take, for example, the preface to *The Jerusalem Sinner Saved*, written by the editor George Offor, who claims:

> That Bunyan, who considered himself one of the most notorious of Jerusalem sinners, should write with the deepest earnestness upon this subject, is not surprising. He had preached upon it with very peculiar pleasure, and, doubtless, from many texts; and, as he says, 'through God's grace, with great success.' It is not probable that, with his characteristic intensity of feeling, and holy fervour in preaching, he ever delivered the same sermon twice; but this was a subject so in unison with his own feelings and experience, that he must have dilated upon it with even unusual interest and earnestness.[14]

Bunyan proves this to be true when, shortly into this work, he writes to his readers:

> We gain this observation:—*That Jesus Christ would have mercy offered, in the first place, to the biggest sinners.*

> That these Jerusalem sinners were the biggest sinners that ever were in the world, I think none will deny, that believes that Christ was the best man that ever was in the world, and also was their Lord God. And that they were to have the first offer of his grace, the text is as clear as the sun; for it saith, 'Beginning at Jerusalem.' 'Preach,' saith he, 'repentance and remission of sins' to the Jerusalem sinners: to the Jerusalem sinners in the *first* place. One would a-thought, since the Jerusalem sinners were the worst and greatest sinners, Christ's greatest enemies, and those that not only despised his person, doctrine, and miracles, but that a little before had had their hands up to the elbows in his heart-blood, that he should rather have said, Go into all the world, and preach repentance and remission of sins among all nations; and after that offer the same to Jerusalem; yea, it had been infinite grace, if he had said so. But what grace is this, or what name shall we give it, when he commands that this repentance and remission of sins, which is designed to be preached in all nations, should first be offered to Jerusalem, in the first place to the worst of sinners![15]

---

14. John Bunyan, *The Jerusalem Sinner Saved*, *Works*, 1:67.
15. Ibid., 70-71.

Bunyan knew the amazing grace of God reaches to even the most vile and deplorable dregs of society because he himself had once been one of those deplorables. Yes, 'His language is that of the heart, fervent but not exaggerated, strong but a plain tale of real feelings.'[16] He knew the grace of God firsthand, but so too did he know the depravity of man's condition. Thus, he could write and preach 'as a dying man to dying men' and as one 'never sure to preach again,' as his contemporary Richard Baxter once said.

His writing and preaching were earnest, urgent, fervent, truthful, striking, loving, warm, and exciting precisely because he knew the gift of God in salvation and the destination of man apart from Christ. Oh, that the Lord would reach down and save more sinners who, with the clarity of Bunyan, would know and believe they were wretches saved by amazing grace! How much more effective our evangelism would become; how much greater our efforts of persuasion when preaching the gospel; how much more certain our own hope in Christ!

---

16. Offor, *Memoir of John Bunyan*, *Works*, 1:xxxii.

CHAPTER 3

The Inescapable Light and Irresistible Grace of Christ: The Tinker's Young Adulthood and Conversion

Evangelist, after he had kissed him, gave him one smile, and bid him God-speed. So he went on with haste, neither spake he to any man by the way; nor, if any asked him, would he vouchsafe them an answer. He went like one that was all the while treading on forbidden ground, and could by no means think himself safe, till again he was got into the way which he left, to follow Mr. Worldly Wiseman's counsel. So, in process of time, Christian got up to the gate. Now, over the gate there was written, 'Knock, and it shall be opened unto you.' [Matt 7:8]

'He that will enter in must first without

Stand knocking at the Gate, nor need he doubt

That is A KNOCKER but to enter in;

For God can love him, and forgive his sin.'

He knocked, therefore, more than once or twice, saying–

'May I now enter here? Will he within

Open to sorry me, though I have been

An undeserving rebel? Then shall I

Not fail to sing his lasting praise on high.'

At last there came a grave person to the gate, named Good-
will, who asked who was there? and whence he came? and
what he would have?

Christian: Here is a poor burdened sinner. I come from the
City of Destruction, but am going to Mount Zion, that I may
be delivered from the wrath to come. I would therefore,
Sir, since I am informed that by this gate is the way thither,
know if you are willing to let me in?

Good-Will: I am willing with all my heart, said he; and with
that he opened the gate.

So when Christian was stepping in, the other gave him
a pull.

(Christian enters through the Wicket-Gate, a symbol of
Christ, in *The Pilgrim's Progress*)

He ran thus till he came at a place somewhat ascending,
and upon that place stood a cross, and a little below, in
the bottom, a sepulchre. So I saw in my dream, that just as
Christian came up with the cross, his burden loosed from
off his shoulders, and fell from off his back, and began to
tumble, and so continued to do, till it came to the mouth of
the sepulchre, where it fell in, and I saw it no more. Then
was Christian glad and lightsome, and said, with a merry
heart, 'He hath given me rest by his sorrow, and life by his
death.' Then he stood still awhile to look and wonder; for
it was very surprising to him, that the sight of the cross
should thus ease him of his burden. He looked therefore,
and looked again, even till the springs that were in his head
sent the waters down his cheeks. [Zech. 12:10] Now, as he
stood looking and weeping, behold three Shining Ones
came to him and saluted him with 'Peace be unto thee'. So
the first said to him, 'Thy sins be forgiven thee' [Mark 2:5];
the second stripped him of his rags, and clothed him with
change of raiment [Zech. 3:4]; the third also set a mark on
his forehead, and gave him a roll with a seal upon it, which

he bade him look on as he ran, and that he should give it in at the Celestial Gate. [Eph. 1:13] So they went their way.

(Christian looks upon the Cross, has his burdened loosed, and is blessed with the benefits of salvation, *The Pilgrim's Progress*)

Conversion is sometimes instantaneous for some. They hear the gospel, and they are immediately drawn to Christ by the power of the Holy Spirit, granted repentance and faith in Christ, and experience the gracious and sovereign act of God's justification over their lives. When such explosive conversions occur, we must praise the Lord for His goodness in seeking and saving the lost (Luke 19:10).

However, it is more often the case that conversion is a gradual process. In fact, the early Puritans saw conversion as a process. This can make tracing a conversion experience rather difficult because God's hand of providence can direct the course of our lives in such a way that, though we do not realize it, some of the events that appeared to be most trivial and insignificant are those events that were most instrumental in watering the seed of the gospel in our hearts.

In this chapter, we will aim to do something quite difficult indeed: Trace Bunyan's conversion experience. This we will do as those who are indebted to the sovereign grace of God, knowing that we cannot see with the perfect clarity that our omniscient Lord can. We acknowledge, as Bunyan stated:

> It would be too long here to stay, to tell you in particular, how God did set me down in all the things of Christ, and how He did, that He might so do, lead me into His words; yea, and also how He did open them unto me, and make them shine before me, and cause them to dwell with me, talk with me, and comfort me over and over, both of His own being, and the being of His Son, and Spirit, and word, and gospel.[1]

While the actual act of salvation is instantaneous, of course, not all sinners experience what may be called an 'instantaneous' conversion. Seldom do men hear the gospel but once and then

---

1. John Bunyan, *Grace Abounding to the Chief of Sinners, Works*, 1:22.

turn to Christ in faith. How many times did the Apostle Paul hear the gospel before Christ finally gripped his heart on the road to Damascus? Indeed, the drawing and wooing of the sinner by God may take some time. Perhaps days, months, and even years may pass before a sinner is finally brought to their knees before the King of kings and Lord of lords to confess Him as their own Lord and Savior.

Bunyan's conversion was very much this latter experience. A large amount of time passed before he bowed the knee to the true King. Though he wrestled regularly with thoughts of damnation and remorse over his sin, he could not defeat his many temptations because he would not, and could not, bow the knee to Christ. His conscience was, in his own words, all but seared and his heart basically hardened. He wrote:

> The thoughts of religion were very grievous to me; I could neither endure it myself, nor that any other should; so that when I have seen some read in those books that concerned Christian piety, it would be as it were a prison to me. Then I said unto God, Depart from me, for I desire not the knowledge of Thy ways. Job xxi. 14, 15. I was now void of all good consideration, heaven and hell were both out of sight and mind; and as for saving and damning, they were least in my thoughts. O Lord, Thou knowest my life, and my ways were not hid from Thee![2]

That God did not utterly and entirely forsake him at this point is a testament to both God's longsuffering, saving grace, and His power to save those whom He has set His affections upon. Yes, as Jesus said, 'All that the Father giveth me shall come to me; and him that cometh to me I will in no wise cast out' (John 6:37). The Father, from eternity past, had promised the young Tinker to His Son, and so Jesus would have this Bunyan for Himself.

Though John's heart had been hardened through a long adolescence of great sinning, the Lord is able to take even the hardest of hearts and pierce them through with the truth of His gospel (Ezek. 36:24-26; Jer. 31:31-34). Though the details of our own conversion testimonies may differ, every true testimony will include a great deal of humility and thankfulness for

---

2. Ibid., 7.

the sovereign grace of God that can turn hardened hearts of stone into soft, pliable hearts of flesh. Rotten corpses though we be, spiritually speaking, and pile of dry bones beyond all earthly hope and in the throngs of eternal despair, Christ is able to save us still through the regenerating work of the Holy Spirit (Ezek. 37). This was Bunyan's own experience and, I pray, either the reader's own experience, or soon to be the reader's experience.

So, what were the steps of Bunyan's conversion? In this chapter, we will trace the Tinker's first-hand account of his life through his entrance into adulthood, his joining the English Civil War, his marriage to his first wife, and his joining of a church. In between, many other events will be examined as part of his journey to Christ.

The Grace of Loss

There is often a great deal of debate surrounding the concept of when exactly a boy becomes a man. Is it when he reaches adolescence? Is it an age, like thirteen? Sixteen? Eighteen? Twenty-one? Is it when his father says he is? When he learns to drive? When he finishes school and starts his first job? When he's married and starts a family?

Answering such a question for another is equally difficult. For Bunyan, in the mid-seventeenth century, his entrance into adulthood likely came in 1642, when at age sixteen his mother and sister died only a month apart from one another. Previously, when he was about nine, he had been plagued by thoughts and 'nightmares and spasms of conscience [which] frightened him and made him wish that there was no such thing as hell.'[3] The death of his mother and sister must have brought these thoughts and nightmares to the forefront of his mind, once more forcing him to confront the reality of his own mortality and those around him. With the death of close loved ones, there was no escaping the reality that, deep down, Bunyan knew that he would one day die and be met with the judgment of God.

---

3. Joel R. Beeke and Paul M. Smalley, *John Bunyan and the Grace of Fearing God* (Philipsburg: P&R Publishing, 2016), 3.

In Psalm 90:12, the Psalmist wrote, 'So teach us to number our days, that we may apply our hearts unto wisdom.' An event like this would have been instrumental in teaching the young Tinker of his own mortality and limited number of days upon the earth. The teacher of Ecclesiastes 7:2-3 was correct to write, 'It is better to go to the house of mourning, than to go to the house of feasting: for that is the end of all men; and the living will lay it to his heart. Sorrow is better than laughter: for by the sadness of the countenance the heart is made better.' The young Tinker had long spent his days in frivolous activities, but now he found himself in the house of mourning, forced to confront his deepest fears and besetting sins. What would become of his soul when he died?

During his youth and teen years, Bunyan was often tormented and fiercely assailed by terrible visions in the night of God's judgment, demonic creatures, and despair. It is possible that the death of his mother and sister aggravated these night terrors once more. George Offor, quoting the writing of Bunyan's 1692 biography, recorded that:

> The first thing that sensibly touched him in this his unregenerate state, were fearful dreams, and visions of the night, which often made him cry out in his sleep, and alarm the house, as if somebody was about to murder him, and being waked, he would start, and stare about him with such a wildness, as if some real apparition had yet remained; and generally those dreams were about evil spirits, in monstrous shapes and forms, that presented themselves to him in threatening postures, as if they would have taken him away, or torn him in pieces. At some times they seemed to belch flame, at other times a continuous smoke, with horrible noises and roaring. Once he dreamed he saw the face of the heavens, as it were, all on fire; the firmament crackling and shivering with the noise of mighty thunders, and an archangel flew in the midst of heaven, sounding a trumpet, and a glorious throne was seated in the east, whereon sat one in brightness, like the morning star, upon which he, thinking it was the end of the world, fell upon his knees, and, with uplifted hands towards heaven, cried, O Lord God, have mercy upon me! What shall I do, the day of judgment is come, and I am not prepared! When immediately he heard a voice behind him, exceeding loud, saying, Repent. At another time he dreamed that he was in a pleasant place, jovial and rioting, banqueting

and feasting his senses, when a mighty earthquake suddenly rent the earth, and made a wide gap, out of which came bloody flames, and the figures of men tossed up in globes of fire, and falling down again with horrible cries, shrieks, and execrations, whilst some devils that were mingled with them, laughed aloud at their torments; and whilst he stood trembling at this sight, he thought the earth sunk under him, and a circle of flame enclosed him; but when he fancied he was just at the point to perish, one in white shining raiment descended, and plucked him out of that dreadful place; whilst the devils cried after him, to leave him with them, to take the just punishment his sins had deserved, yet he escaped the danger, and leaped for joy when he awoke and found it was a dream.[4]

Perhaps the reader can relate to Bunyan's fear of impending doom and judgment.[5] God has often employed the most ordinary of experiences in the most extraordinary of ways to bring about the conversion of His saints. Consider how Charles Spurgeon's conversion was centered around entering a small country church on a snowy day to hear the Word of God expounded; recall how Martin Luther's conversion was, in some ways, dependent upon a lightning storm which struck such fear in his heart, he swore to become a monk; remember how John Newton (famed author of *Amazing Grace*) was ultimately led to Christ through the difficulties, trials, terrors, and hardships of being a sailor. Is it really any surprise that God could also use something as simple as nightmares to impart some measure of grace to a sinner?

Such nightmares would have been instrumental in not only chasing the Tinker to Christ, but also preparing him for his later and great allegorical tales. Offor notes, 'Such dreams as these fitted him in after life to be the glorious dreamer of the Pilgrim's Progress, in which a dream is told which doubtless embodies some of those which terrified him in the night visions of his youth.'[6] Before his conversion, his imagination

---

4. George Offor, *Memoir of John Bunyan, Works,* 1:v.

5. The author of this little work certainly can. One of the Lord's graces in my own conversion was the use of reoccurring night terrors, which exhorted me to tenaciously flee from my sin and cling to the Lord Jesus Christ. Such testimonies are not uncommon.

6. Ibid. George Offor, *Memoir of John Bunyan, Works,* 1:v.

was like a curse, constantly threatening and terrifying him. But, after conversion, his imagination was baptized in the grace of God, sanctified by the indwelling of the Holy Spirit, and able to be utilized for the glory of God and the advancement of His Kingdom.

Yet, it was the death of his mother and sister that brought a time of deep sorrow, through which John was reminded of his own mortality. His father remarried soon after, and, in 1644, Bunyan would join the army and fight in the English Civil War. It was during this time that the young man would experience another act of God's common grace over his life.[7]

The Common Grace of Near-Death Experiences

That God will often miraculously spare the lives of His people is well known and understood by most. King Hezekiah, when he prayed that the Lord might spare his life, was granted fifteen years longer to live (2 Kings 20:5-6). When on the battlefield, exhausted and cornered by Ishbibenob—a son of the giants—David's life was spared when Abishai, son of Zeruiah, struck the Philistine down (2 Sam. 21:15-17). Saints throughout the history of Christendom have often attested to the many occasions wherein they *should* have died but, by some invisible hand of providence, their lives were spared. This is none other than the divine providence of God in action.

But does God spare those who do not belong to Him? Will He spare the lives of those most heinous and destructive of sinners? The answer is obviously yes, and especially when He intends to turn those sinners to saints.

Bunyan's life is a testament to God's common grace in sparing the life of sinners. Every day that a person's life is sustained is, of course, an act of God's grace. To think, even the atheist who mocks and taunts the Creator of the universe is upheld by the Word of the Creator's power (Heb. 1:3)! Since there is none that seeks God, there is none that is worthy of

---

7. While I recognize that grace itself is not 'common' in the sense that it is not deserved, I use the term 'common grace' to distinguish from 'saving grace.' 'Common grace' is experienced by all men as God causes it to rain on the just and unjust alike (Matt. 5:45). 'Special grace' is that grace that only Christians experience in their conversion to Christ.

life. But God mercifully upholds the creation by His sovereign power. On occasion, though we often neglect the worship of God for His common grace in this area, there are moments wherein His grace is evidenced and seen clearly by even the most hardened of sinners. Typically, such moments are met with scorn and laughter, or idolatrous statements like, 'The universe was looking out for me back there.' But, as Bunyan attested, the work of preserving his life, even as a sinner, was not the universe's work, but the sole work and grace of God Almighty, the Creator of the heavens and the earth.

Bunyan once wrote of his time as a sinful youth that the Lord did not utterly forsake him, but continued to work upon his heart, 'not now with convictions, but judgments; yet such as were mixed with mercy.'[8] He describes how, through a series of near-death experiences, the Lord both spared and sustained his life and, through these moments, tugged at his young and sin-gripped heart.

On one occasion, he described how, 'I fell into a creek of the sea, and hardly escaped drowning.'[9] Hardly the last time he faced near death in deep waters, he also described how, 'Another time I fell out of a boat into Bedford river, but, mercy yet preserved me alive.'[10] On yet another occasion, the young Tinker was in a field with a friend when he spotted a venomous snake. He described how, 'I having a stick in my hand, struck her over the back; and having stunned her, I forced open her mouth with my stick, and plucked her sting out with my fingers; by which act had not God been merciful unto me, I might by my desperateness, have brought myself to my end.'[11]

Perhaps these occasions read as little more than the playtime adventures of a rambunctious youth, no more dangerous than the trifles that all other children often get themselves into. But Bunyan, in his own peculiar way, was able to look back over his life before conversion and recognize that it was not blind chance, or luck, that had preserved his life and

---

8. John Bunyan, *Grace Abounding to the Chief of Sinners*, *Works*, 1:7.

9. Ibid.

10. Ibid.

11. Ibid.

directed his course. He knew that it was the Lord who had protected him.

The most profound moment of near death came after John, at around age eighteen, had joined the army. It was likely 1645, at the siege of Leicester, about two or three years after the death of his mother and sister, when John experienced his closest brush with death.[12] It is possible that other moments like this one had occurred and he forgot them, or did not pay them any mind, but this event was one that caught his attention. He wrote:

> This also I have taken notice of, with thanksgiving: When I was a soldier, I with others, were drawn out to go to such a place to besiege it; but when I was just ready to go, one of the company desired to go in my room: to which, when I had consented, he took my place; and coming to the siege, as he stood sentinel, he was shot in the head with a musket-bullet and died.[13]

The young Tinker experienced one brush with death after the next, but this one appears to have been a sort of wake-up call for the poor wretch. Had he gone out into battle, as he was supposed to, then it would have been his own head shot through with a musket-bullet. Again, this was not the blind movements of fate, but the sovereign Lord directing Bunyan's paths and preserving his life. As the Lord would have it, the Tinker's life would be extended because he would be given to the Son of God, and he would be used for the glory of God.

Yet, despite each of these close encounters with death, none moved him to repentance and faith. Still more time would need to pass, and more experiences with God's sovereign grace, before he would be drawn, fully and finally, to the Savior of his soul.

Life and Grace During the English Civil War

During Bunyan's time in the English Civil War, he encountered serious Puritan thought and preaching in a way he had not

---

12. See the editor's footnotes, Bunyan, *Grace Abounding to the Chief of Sinners, Works*, 1:7.

13. Ibid.

previously as he fought alongside Puritans willing to die for their beliefs. The war would prove to be a long and bloody affair, spanning nine years, during which casualties would climb to about 200,000 soldiers and civilians. Referring to it as the English Civil War (singular) may be somewhat misleading, as this time of warfare spanned three civil wars (plural) in a nine-year period. When the Tinker entered the war in 1644, he joined with the forces of Parliament, which would later be rebranded as the New Model Army under Oliver Cromwell. This employment hardly changed his economic status for, 'He served in the garrison at Newport Pagnell, a unit that was "chronically behind in its pay and poorly equipped."'[14]

The war was, itself, an intriguing array of interconnected and tangled threads. Motivations could change and differ from week to week, with new groups entering the fray and others changing allegiances and switching sides frequently.

The first steps toward war were taken when King James I died in 1625, and his son, King Charles I, became the new king. Historians John Woodbridge and Frank James III explain that the Puritans greeted the new king rather unfavorably for two reasons: He believed in the Divine Right of Kings, the idea that kings are 'little Gods on Earth,' and he also, almost immediately upon taking the throne, 'married a Roman Catholic princess, Henrietta-Marie de Bourbon, which raised the specter of a Roman Catholic heir to the English throne.'[15] Charles I's stance on the divine-right of Kings, his marriage to a Roman Catholic, and other anti-Puritan measures were entirely counterintuitive and antithetical to all that the Reformation had stood for.

Vitriol and antagonism grew and spread between the Puritans and the king, as he then appointed William Laud as archbishop of Canterbury in 1633. Laud held to High Anglicanism, 'with its sacramental emphasis on ceremonies

---

14. Joel R. Beeke and Paul M. Smalley, *John Bunyan and the Grace of Fearing God* (Phillipsburg: P&R Publishing, 2016), 4. See also: Richard L. Greaves, 'Bunyan, John,' in *ODNB*, 8:702.

15. John D. Woodbridge and Frank A. James III, *Church History Volume Two: From Pre-Reformation to the Present Day* (Grand Rapids: Zondervan, 2013), 266.

and a theological inclination toward Arminianism.'[16] The Reformed theology of the Puritans was under attack. Therefore, matters only grew more heated between the king and Parliament because Parliament was comprised of mostly English Puritans at the time.

The true trouble began to brew when, in 1637, Charles I attempted to 'impose on the Scottish Church a new Anglican version of the prayer book...'[17] For the Scottish Church and the English Puritans, this was too much. Woodbridge and James III note that the Scots had some interesting reactions to the King's new imposition:

> One Scottish wag called it the 'vomit of Romish superstition.' When Jenny Geddes, a vegetable seller, heard the dean of St. Giles Cathedral in Edinburg read from the new prayer book, she stood up and threw her 'creepie-stool' (a folding stool) directly at his head. As she hurled the stool, she is reported to have yelled: 'Devil cause you colic in your stomach, false thief: dare you say the Mass in my ear?'[18]

For the Scottish Church and English Puritans, the continued Reformation of the Church relied on the purging of all popish rituals, doctrines, and superstitions from the Bride of Christ's worship and assemblies.

This would lead directly into what is known as the Bishop Wars, during which Edinburgh experienced rioting, Scots signed the Nation Covenant in blood, and the nation made it clear that they would sooner 'die before submitting to Anglicanism.'[19] Two military campaigns were led, but the Scots proved to be too much for Charles I.

Unsurprisingly, the mostly Puritan Parliament was no supporter of the king, either. When the Scottish Army advanced upon England and threatened to march south upon them, the king attempted to rally support through Parliament. But they had only grown more antagonistic toward the king. When called together, Parliament enacted a law that the king

16. Ibid.
17. Ibid.
18. Ibid.
19. Ibid.

could not dissolve its meeting without its consent, creating what became known as the 'Long Parliament.' They would, technically, meet for twenty years, from 1640 to 1660, with no one possessing the power to dissolve their meeting.

The king was not at all pleased with Parliament and actually began to accuse some members of treason, believing they had conspired with the Scots to invade England and destroy the Crown. 'The traitors were identified, and Charles, accompanied by four hundred soldiers, dramatically burst into the House of Commons in January 1642, only to find the five had fled.'[20] The king, fearing for the safety of his own life and that of his family, soon fled. The Civil War had officially begun.

The first part of the war was waged from 1642 to 1646, and the first battle occurred at Edgehill in October of 1642. There was no clear victor in this first battle, but the Royalist forces of the Crown would prove to be too much for the forces of Parliament. So, the Long Parliament did what the king had formerly accused them of: They entered an alliance with the Scots, which would prove to bring them a great deal of success. At Marston Moor, in July of 1644, Parliamentary forces won their first important victory. It was of this victory over the Royalist forces that Oliver Cromwell famously said, 'God made them as stubble to our swords.'[21]

Cromwell became a more prominent figure after this, when he restructured some of the Parliamentary forces into the New Model Army. This army, which Bunyan was serving in, was made up of not just Puritans, but Independents and Congregationalists. They also proved to be too much for the Royalists. Charles I was left with no choice but to surrender in May of 1646.

But there was a twist stranger than fiction: Charles I negotiated with the Scots, and they agreed to help Royalist forces on the condition that, upon success, Presbyterianism would be adopted for at least three years in both Scotland and England. Thus, the second war was fought from 1648 to 1649, and was decisively concluded in August, 1649. Here, Cromwell

20. Ibid.
21. Ibid., 267.

once more defeated the Royalists, now joined with the Scots, at the Battle of Preston.

The battle was still not over, however. The Long Parliament was still in session, and though Cromwell had defeated the Royalist forces of Charles I, there was a real risk that he would be reinstalled as king. While Cromwell and his New Model Army were mostly Independents and Congregationalists, Parliament was mostly Anglicans and Presbyterians. So, Cromwell marched on Parliament and barred the Anglicans and Presbyterians from entering. Only Independents were admitted. Those who were barred from entrance, who would not leave, about forty-five, were arrested. This event, known as 'Pride's Purge,' saw around 370 members of Parliament denied entrance, and only around 100 admitted in.[22]

This new 'purged' Parliament, remembered as 'The Rump Parliament,' put Charles I on trial and had him executed for treason. Thus, the final of the three civil wars was begun when Cromwell then led the New Model Army to fight against the Irish Confederates who had allied themselves with the remaining Royalists. At the same time, the Scots were fearful that Cromwell's government would not long permit Presbyterianism, and so they made Charles II, the son of Charles I, their new king on 23 June, 1650. He appeared favorable to Presbyterianism and signed 'the Solemn League and Covenant,' which was meant to protect Scottish Presbyterianism.

Cromwell and his forces still proved too much for both the Irish and the Scots. The Scots were defeated at the Battle of Inverkeithing in July of 1651, with a final defeat occurring at Worcester in September of that same year. After, Charles II would flee to England, elude capture, and manage to escape to France. Some early estimates, like those of Sir William Perry, held that 618,000 Irish had died, either having been

---

22. See: Woodbridge and James III, *Church History Volume Two: From Pre-Reformation to the Present Day*, 267.

killed in the war, or because of starvation and plague,[23] while thousands of others had gone into exile. [24]

This was the long and bloody war that Bunyan fought in, and fighting on the side of the Parliamentary forces, and later the New Model Army, meant that he was encountering both Puritan and Independent thought and teaching. Though he was not in the war long, he was regularly surrounded by those men who rejected High Anglicanism, the imposition of the *Book of Common Prayer,* and held the Bible in high regard. These were men who were willing to die for their faith in Christ and would die to see the sins of popish Romanism purged from the church. While the Magisterial Reformers had been called home to the celestial city decades before, Bunyan was being influenced by a new group of Reformers in his own day.

During this time of warfare, there was also a great deal of movement amongst the Particular Baptists that would also be influential to Bunyan. Back in Bedford, Benjamin Coxe preached for a short time in the 1640's. In 1646, this same Coxe became one of the signees of the second edition of the First London Baptist Confession of Faith. This meant that both Bunyan and Bedford were being introduced to the Puritanism of the Particular Baptist movement, making them susceptible to adopting such teachings and doctrines as their own.

After his short foray into the war and time spent away, it was time for the young Tinker to return home and settle down with a wife of his own.

Marriage as a Means of Grace?

Protestants reject the Roman Catholic dogma that marriage is one of seven sacraments that God has bestowed upon

---

23. Charles Carlton, *Going to the Wars: The Experience of the British Civil Wars, 1638-1631* (London, UK: Routledge, 1992), 212-13.) More modern estimates are still quite high, believing that between the war, plague, starvation, and exile, between 15-20% of Ireland's population was ravaged.

24. According to Micheál Ó Siochrú, "Between 1649 and 1653 Ireland suffered a 'demographic catastrophe', with mortality in the region of 20 per cent due to the continued fighting, alongside widespread starvation and disease." Micheál Ó Siochrú, 'Atrocity, Codes of Conduct and the Irish in the British Civil Wars 1641-1653', Past & Present 195:1 (2007), 80.) Even these more conservative estimates are still startling. Ireland surrendered in 1653.

the Church. In fact, Anglican and Reformed Protestants recognize only two sacraments, or ordinances, as a means of grace within the Church: Baptism and the Lord's Supper. But Protestants do put a great deal of emphasis on marriage, and rightfully so. After all, it is through the marriage union of husband and wife that the marriage of Christ and His Bride, the Church, is pictured for the world (Eph. 5:22–6:3). It is also by this union that husbands model the leadership and love of Christ for their wives and children, wives lovingly submit to the leadership of their husbands as Christ did to the Father during the incarnation, and children are discipled by their parents to follow Christ all the days of their life. Eventually, Bunyan's household would model this supreme example of Christ-likeness, shining as a bright light within an almost bleak cosmos. But before his conversion, it was his first wife (and her family) which had a sobering effect on the young Tinker.

After returning from the war, Bunyan tells of how he became a married man. The year was 1649, and the Puritans had just put Charles I on trial for treason, effectively establishing a commonwealth, rather than a monarchy. The English Civil War would, of course, continue. But, for the Tinker, this was a time to settle down. He was about twenty-one years old when he married, and exceptionally poor. Not very much is known of his first wife. Eventually, they would be blessed with the birth of a child, Mary, whose baptism would take place on 20 July, 1650. She would, however, be born blind. Though his first wife's name is not recorded, it is thought by some that her name may have been Mary since that was the name chosen for their first child.

Bunyan loved his wife and children. They were, as he put it, mercies from the Lord. His first wife, especially, was another act of God's grace in his life, for her father was a pious and holy man. Though apparently dead by the time they married, stories of her father's piety influenced the Tinker. Likewise, though she was as poor as he was, she did possess two books from her father that would play an instrumental role in guiding John to the true Christian faith. The Tinker records how:

My mercy was, to light upon a wife whose father was counted godly: This woman and I, though we came together as poor as poor might be (not having so much household stuff as a dish or a spoon betwixt us both), yet this she had for her part: The Plain Man's Pathway to Heaven and The Practice of Piety; which her father had left her when he died. In these two books I would sometimes read with her, wherein I also found some things that were somewhat pleasing to me (but all this while I met with no conviction).[25]

The Plain Man's Pathway to Heaven details, through the conversation of four men, the gospel and the Christian life. *The Practice of Piety* was very similar, but designed with the purpose of making sure the saint was not caught as a thief in the night at the return of Christ. While he claims the reading of these works met with no conviction, it is clear that there was an act of God's grace taking place. Rather than turning away from the books, selling them for scraps, or even burning them (as some sinners are prone to do with godly books), he continued to read them with a great deal of interest.

His wife's own example should not be overlooked either. Of his first wife, he notes how, 'She also would be often telling of me what a godly man her father was, and how he would reprove and correct vice, both in his house, and among his neighbours; what a strict and holy life he lived in his days, both in word and deed.'[26] The result was not conversion, but the speech of his wife and the reading of these books, 'did beget within me some desires to religion: so that because I knew no better, I fell in very eagerly with the religion of the times; to wit, to go to church twice a day, and that too with the foremost; and there should very devoutly, both say and sing, as others did, yet retaining my wicked life...'[27] As the Apostle Paul once wrote in 1 Corinthians 7:16, 'For what knowest thou, O wife, whether thou shalt save thy husband? or how knowest thou, O man, whether thou shalt save thy wife?' While his first wife may not have known it, her influence left an indelible impression upon her husband.

---

25. Bunyan, *Grace Abounding to the Chief of Sinners*, *Works*, 1:7.
26. Ibid.
27. Ibid.

Yet, he could not escape some of the broad superstitions of his own day. Though he served with the Independents/Congregationalists of Cromwell's New Model Army, he seems to have held to some form of superstition at this time as well, for he wrote:

> I was so over-run with the spirit of superstition, that I adored, and that with great devotion, even all things (both the high-place, priest, clerk, vestment, service, and what else) belonging to the church; counting all things holy that were therein contained, and especially, the priest and clerk most happy, and without doubt, greatly blessed, because they were the servants, as I then thought, of God, and were principal in the holy temple, to do His work therein.[28]

What Bunyan describes here is the common experience of many a man. While no true conviction of sin had yet taken place, and thus no conversion, he was fascinated by the rituals and ordinances of the English Church. When he looked at the services held within the church, he thought himself to be amongst the holy of holies and, for being in their presence, to have received some merit of mercy and grace through them. Looking to those who preached and taught the Word, with their vestment and offices, he even believed them to be the most blessed of the Lord, having been chosen to do the work of God within His holy temple.

A desire for religion was awakened with him, but he instead found superstition. He played the role of what one may describe as a nominal Christian. He attended services, heard the sermons, sang the song, and prayed the prayers, but there was no spiritual awakening that had yet taken place. While God was wooing and drawing the young husband and father to Himself, more time would still elapse before his conversion.

The Grace of a Still Small Voice

Bunyan's testimony in *Grace Abounding* takes a slightly unusual and very unexpected turn when he writes about how, after his conscience was wounded by a Sunday sermon, and his best

---

28. Ibid.

delights 'benumbed,' he went to play a game of cat.[29] His mind had been tormented by the sermon of the pastor, who had spoken at length of the evils of breaking the Sabbath, but some time had passed, and Bunyan's heart had settled.

As he played his game, and was about to strike the 'cat' a second time:

> A voice did suddenly dart from heaven into my soul, which said, Wilt thou leave thy sins and go to heaven, or have thy sins and go to hell? At this I was put to an exceeding maze; wherefore leaving my cat upon the ground, I looked up to heaven, and was, as if I had, with the eyes of my understanding, seen the Lord Jesus looking down upon me, as being very hotly displeased with me, and as if He did severely threaten me with some grievous punishment for these and other ungodly practices.[30]

Some may find this encounter incredible, and even hard to believe, but the Tinker does not appear to have been one prone for exaggerations in his own life. Though such an event may seem fantastical, it is one that had a great impact on John. While the effects of the sermon upon his own heart were powerful, yet short-lived, this still small voice (1 Kings 19:12), spoken directly to his heart, pierced through him.

Perhaps this was not God speaking directly to Bunyan, but God stirring up his mind and thoughts to recall something he had heard in the sermon that same morning. Whatever the case, the question, 'Wilt thou leave thy sins and go to heaven, or have thy sins and go to hell?' led him into a fit of amazement. He understood, at least momentarily, that God was truly angry with him for his sin and there was no

---

29. Cat, also sometimes called 'tip-cat,' appears to have been a precursor to cricket. The basic idea was that a stick, about three feet long, was to be used as a bat and a piece of wood, about six inches long and two inches thick, called the 'cat,' was to be placed on the ground. This piece of wood would then be struck so that it would rise into the air. The player was then to strike it. If he missed, he was out. If he hit it, there appears to have been two variations to the game. The first was that he would call out a number for how far he hit it, and if he guessed correctly, he would score a point and play again. Other versions have a four-sided 'cat' with numbers on each side to determine the scoring. Still other versions have the player attempting to round bases before the 'cat' is thrown to home base. See: George Offor's footnotes to *Grace Abounding*, *Works*, 1:8. Also, see entry on 'tip-cat' in Encyclopedia Britannica.

30. Bunyan, *Grace Abounding to the Chief of Sinners*, *Works*, 1:8.

escaping the judgment of God. As the writer of Hebrews said, 'Neither is there any creature that is not manifest in his sight: but all things are naked and opened unto the eyes of him with whom we have to do' (Heb. 4:13). In that moment, when Bunyan was preparing to strike the 'cat' a second time, he was struck the second time that day by the judgment of God. It was as though he were being pierced through by God's gaze upon his soul.

What was the man to do? Would he now repent and turn to Christ and have heaven, or would he refuse?

Unfortunately, as strange as the event may be, Bunyan's reaction is perhaps stranger still: He doubled down in his sin. This was not, however, the brash rejection of God that one may expect an arrogant sinner to make. No, this was the sorrowful decision of a sinner that felt to be beyond all hope. In his own words, 'This conclusion was fastened on my spirit (for the former hint did set my sins again before my face), That I had been a great and grievous sinner, and that it was now too late for me to look after heaven; for Christ would not forgive me, nor pardon my transgressions.'[31] This was, of course, wrong. God would forgive him if he'd simply repent of his sin and turn to Christ in faith. But these deep feelings of despair were not lost on Bunyan and they are one of the many reasons why he would preach, speak, and write directly and often to those who felt themselves to be the worst of sinners, that they would know the hope of the true offer of the gospel. He had felt the shame and despair and had been deceived by Satan for long enough into believing that Christ would not have him. When he later discovered that Christ invites even the most wretched of sinners to come and seek forgiveness in His name, Bunyan would make it his mission to declare this great and wonderful truth to others.

But, at this point, the despair was only just beginning. Some of the saddest words that Bunyan penned describe this sad state of affairs when he wrote:

> I felt my heart sink in despair, concluding it was too late; and therefore I resolved in my mind I would go on in sin: for, thought I, if the case be thus, my state is surely miserable;

---

31. Ibid.

miserable if I leave my sins, and but miserable if I follow them; I can but be damned, and if I must be so, I had as good be damned for many sins, as be damned for few.[32]

When the Apostle Paul asked his rhetorical question, 'What shall we say then? Shall we continue in sin, that grace may abound?' (Rom. 6:1), his response was, 'God forbid. How shall we, that are dead to sin, live any longer therein?' (Rom. 6:2). But one cannot help but wonder how he would have reacted to a statement like Bunyan's. Probably, if anyone had said, 'Paul, I will continue to sin, and that greatly, because Christ will not have me and all that is left is hell. I may as well sin greatly if I already be damned,' Paul's answer would have been, 'God forbid!'

Bunyan had not yet tasted of the goodness of God's saving grace, but he was certainly beginning to get a taste of God's judgment against sin. His reaction may even read as though he were a nihilist, saying, 'I may as well eat, drink, and be merry, for tomorrow I die!' (Eccles. 8:15, Isa. 22:13, 1 Cor. 15:32). Maybe this was close to what he was thinking in his heart of hearts.

His actual heart at the time was a swarming pit of darkness and shadowy despair. He would go on to write of his desperation that:

> I returned desperately to my sport again; and I well remember, that presently this kind of despair did so possess my soul, that I was persuaded I could never attain to other comfort than what I should get in sin; for heaven was gone already, so that on that I must not think; wherefore I found within me great desire to take my fill of sin, still studying what sin was yet to be committed, that I might taste the sweetness of it; and I made as much haste as I could to fill my belly with its delicates, lest I should die before I had my desire; for that I feared greatly.[33]

It is not that Bunyan wanted to die and go to hell, but that he was so very fearful of hell, and dreaded the thought of dying and facing God's judgment for an eternity so very much, that he thought his only comfort in life and death would be found in committing as many great sins as he could. He believed,

---

32. Ibid.
33. Ibid., 8-9.

at this time, that the sins he committed during his mortal life would be the only pleasures he would experience in all his eternity.

How sad a state to be in! To believe that oneself is beyond the reach of Christ's mighty and strong arms to save is a dreadful estate to be ensnared within indeed. Yet, this is where this poor wretch found himself. And, so, he began to commit more and more sins, searching out, with desperation, those acts of depravity that had still yet to be committed.

Bunyan attests, 'In these things, I protest before God, I lye not, neither do I feign this form of speech; these were really, strongly, and with all my heart, my desires: The good Lord, Whose mercy is unsearchable, forgive me my transgressions!'[34]

The Grace of God in Shame

Many of us have examples from our own lives when, at one point, we felt deep shame and contrition for having been caught sinning. By the grace of God, these moments of shame will, on occasion, lead to a genuine repentance of sin and faith in Jesus.

For Bunyan, such a moment came when he was caught cursing and swearing by a woman who was herself no example of piety and righteousness. After having decided that the Lord was unable to save him, and that there was no room in heaven for such a great sinner as he, he took it upon himself to play the madman in public. Cursing and swearing with his tongue, his speech became that of the grave; rotten and putrid.

This manner of living continued with him for about a month after his experience while playing cat. Then, one day, the Lord brought a crushing end to this manner of life. Bunyan remembered how he was outside a shop window, cursing and swearing as was his usual custom, when suddenly he was rebuked from the least likely of sources: A woman that he, at the time, thought even more deplorable than he. He recorded this interaction by writing:

> There sate within, the woman of the house, and heard me; who, though she also was a very loose and ungodly wretch, yet

34. Ibid., 1:8.

protested that I swore and cursed at that most fearful rate, that she was made to tremble to hear me; and told me further, that I was the ungodliest fellow for swearing, that she ever heard in all her life; and that I, by thus doing, was able to spoil all the youth in the whole town, if they come but in my company.[35]

How unexpected! If ever there was a woman that he would have thought he could speak loosely around, it would have been she! She herself bore a reputation of being very loose and ungodly (likely, he meant, with her tongue), yet she was flabbergasted and appalled by the Tinker's own promiscuous language.

Probably, what really hurt the Tinker's pride, was her claim that he was the most ungodly fellow, and that he would spoil all the youth in town. Did the accusation make him think of his own sweet Mary at home? Did he consider the ungodly impact he might be having upon her? Had he not wished that his own father had been of a godlier caliber, that he may not have learned such great wickedness as a child? Was the son not now following in the sins of the father? Still, this moment would play another vital role in causing John to leave and forsake his sin in favor of pursuing Christ.

He explained how, after this rebuke from one as ungodly as he, he could only fall silent and hang his head in shame. He wrote, also, how he felt not only 'secret shame,' but, 'that too, as I thought, before the God of heaven.'[36] It was at this point he wished that his father may have been one more godly, and more prone to discipline his children for their sins, that he would never have learned to curse in such a manner with his tongue.

While it seemed impossible at first, John determined, from this point on, to leave off and forsake his swearing and cursing. The reformation of his character did not occur overnight, but, as he attested, it *did* occur. However, true conversion was not yet attained, for his obedience to God was almost all but outward. His diseased and hardened heart remained within his spirit; pricked often by his failure to keep the Law, but never pierced completely through with gospel truth.

---

35. Ibid., 9.
36. Ibid.

During this time of outward reformation and superstitious piety, he met a man who taught him to take interest in the reading of the Bible. This man spoke well and pleasantly of the Scriptures, which perked up the Tinker's ears. Two things happened within this acquaintanceship: First, in reading of the Scriptures, Bunyan recognized that it is a pleasure to read the Bible. He wrote, 'I betook me to my Bible, and began to take great pleasure in reading, but especially with the historical part thereof; for as for Paul's Epistles, and such like Scriptures, I could not away with them, being as yet ignorant, either of the corruptions of my nature, or of the want and worth of Jesus Christ to save me.'[37] Second, Bunyan's pride began to flare up. For, during this time, as he tried his best to keep the commandments, he truly began to feel it within his power to fulfill the Law of God. He wrote how, when it came to keeping the Commandments, 'yet now and then [I] should break one, and so afflict my conscience; but then I should repent, and say, I was sorry for it, and promise God to do better next time, and there get help again; for then I thought I pleased God as well as any man in England.'[38]

Those around him were often fooled by his new display of outward morality, seeing this as 'my great conversion, from prodigious profaneness, to something like a moral life.'[39] They began to outwardly praise Bunyan, both to his face and behind his back, believing him to truly have experienced the inner working of God's grace. But outward appearances can be deceiving, and Bunyan admitted, 'yet I knew not Christ, nor grace, nor faith, nor hope; for, as I have well seen since, had I then died, my state had been most fearful.'[40]

The words of those around Bunyan were, no doubt, meant to exhort and encourage him in greater holiness. Instead, they had the unfortunate effect of increasing his already great pridefulness. He confessed:

> But oh! when I understood these were their words and opinions
> of me, it pleased me mighty well. For, though as yet I was

---

37. Ibid.
38. Ibid.
39. Ibid.
40. Ibid.

nothing but a poor painted hypocrite, yet, I loved to be talked of as one that was truly godly. I was proud of my godliness, and indeed, I did all I did, either to be seen of, or to be well spoken of, by men: and thus I continued for about a twelvemonth, or more.[41]

The true work of conversion was only just beginning for the Tinker.

The Grace of God in Overheard Conversations

During this time of moral reformation and outward displays of prideful piety, there were still certain sins and habits that John had a difficult time abandoning. How much easier a time he would have had if he had simply turned to Christ for forgiveness and salvation! As it was, he tried to do all in his own power to put off his own sins and struggled terribly.

One of his own perceived sins was that of ringing the church bells. 'I had taken much delight in ringing, but my conscience beginning to be tender, I thought such practice was but vain, and therefore forced myself to leave it; yet my mind hankered; wherefore I would go to the steeple house, and look on, though I durst not ring.'[42] Over some time, he convinced himself to not even stand near and watch the ringing of the bell any longer, first believing it possible that the bell might fall on him, then convincing himself it was possible a beam would fall on him, and finally thought even the steeple itself might fall and kill him. He wrote, 'I should think again, should the bell fall with a swing, it might first hit the wall, and then, rebounding upon me, might kill me for all this beam...'[43] Then, having made his way to the door, he began to think himself safe. That is, until it occurred to him, 'How if the steeple itself should fall? And this thought (it may for aught I know) when I stood and looked on, did continually so shake my mind, that I durst not stand at the steeple-door

---

41. Ibid., 10.
42. Ibid.
43. Ibid.

any longer, but was forced to flee, for fear the steeple should fall upon my head.'[44]

Thus, one perceived sin was defeated, but still he struggled with another: The perceived sin of dancing. Whatever sort of dancing he was engaged in, it took him a year before he defeated that temptation. But, all the while, his pride rose within. He believed during this time, 'God cannot choose but be now pleased with me; yea, to relate it in mine own way, I thought no man in England could please God better than I.'[45]

This is, perhaps, one of the most miserable estates a sinner can fall into: That of false righteousness, or works-based religion, thinking that not only must salvation be earned, but actually believing that salvation *can* be earned by enough striving and working. But, as the Apostle Paul wrote, 'Knowing that a man is not justified by the works of the law, but by the faith of Jesus Christ, even we have believed in Jesus Christ, that we might be justified by the faith of Christ, and not by the works of the law: for by the works of the law shall no flesh be justified' (Gal. 2:16). This was a lesson yet to be learned, but what a liberty it would bring when he finally did learn it!

As he confessed, 'I was all this while ignorant of Jesus Christ; and going about to establish my own righteousness; and had perished therein, had not God in mercy showed me more of my state by nature.'[46] Praise the Lord that, even in the midst of such great pride, the Lord was still working on the heart of the Tinker.

Eventually, God led him to overhear a conversation amongst women from Pastor John Gifford's congregation (more on him below) that had such a profound impact upon him, he would never forget it and their words would leave him forever changed. It so happened that, one day, he was called into Bedford to do the mechanical work of his profession as a tinker. While there, he happened upon the women and overheard their manner of speech.

> I came where there were three or four poor women sitting at a door, in the sun, talking about the things of God; and

44. Ibid.
45. Ibid.
46. Ibid.

being now willing to hear them discourse, I drew near to hear what they said, for I was now a brisk talker also myself, in the matters of religion; but I may say, I heard but understood not; for they were far above, out of my reach. Their talk was about a new birth, the work of God on their hearts, also how they were convinced of their miserable state by nature; they talked how God had visited their souls with His love in the Lord Jesus, and with what words and promises they had been refreshed, comforted, and supported, against the temptations of the devil: moreover, they reasoned of the suggestions and temptations of Satan in particular; and told to each other, by which they had been afflicted and how they were borne up under his assaults. They also discoursed of their own wretchedness of heart, and of their unbelief; and did contemn, slight and abhor their own righteousness, as filthy, and insufficient to do them any good.[47]

Such speech was, to the Tinker's ears, utterly foreign! Yet, how pleasant their words were. He wrote of them, 'And, methought, they spake as if joy did make them speak; they spake with such pleasantness of scripture language, and with such appearance of grace in all they said, that they were to me, as if they had found a new world; as if they were people that dwelt alone, and were not to be reckoned among their neighbours. Numb. xxiii.9.'[48] Within them he discovered the scent and appearance of those who had been in the presence of Jesus; he met with those who were true citizens of the celestial city.

His own ignorance was laid bare before him, and he recognized he knew nothing of the religion they spoke of so joyfully. Yet, he could not keep himself away. He would regularly return to hear them speak. And, as he did so, he marveled for:

The more I went amongst them, the more I did question my condition; and as I still do remember, presently I found two things within me, at which I did sometimes marvel (especially considering what a blind, ignorant, sordid and ungodly wretch but just before I was). The one was a very great softness and tenderness of heart, which caused me to fall under the conviction of what by scripture they asserted, and the other

47. Ibid.
48. Ibid.

was a great bending in my mind, to a continual meditating on it, and on all other good things, which at any time I heard or read of.[49]

Their holy joy in Christ inspired the Tinker to finally break off his companionship with a friend who was, 'a most wicked creature for cursing, and swearing, and whoreing.'[50] The temptations would not yet cease, but he was nearing an assurance of saving faith in Christ.

His heart, now, was bent on knowing the Lord. His strongest desire was to know the truth of saving faith and salvation in Christ. 'I began to look into the Bible with new eyes, and read as I never did before, and especially the epistles of the apostle St Paul were sweet and pleasant to me; and indeed I was then never out of the Bible, either by reading or meditation; still crying out to God, that I might know the truth, and way to heaven and glory.'[51]

Thus began a long period of searching for faith amid doubts and confusions regarding grace. As he described it, 'Neither as yet could I attain to any comfortable persuasion that I had faith in Christ; but instead of having satisfaction here, I began to find my soul to be assaulted with fresh doubts about my future happiness; especially with such as these, whether I was elected? But how, if the day of grace should now be past and gone?'[52]

Eventually, he would join a church meeting and sit under the teaching of Mr. Gifford in Bedford. It is extremely likely that this group of women, whose overheard conversation had such a profound impact on him, were the same women who invited him into this church fellowship.

The Grace of God in the Writings of Past Saints

Let it not be understated that Bunyan's first wife was paramount in leading him to the Lord. Her gifting him with *The Plain Man's Pathway to Heaven* and *The Practice of Piety*

---

49. Ibid., 11.
50. Ibid.
51. Ibid.
52. Ibid., 1:13.

were instrumental tools in leading him to a church wherein he heard the gospel regularly declared. These books also had the unintended effect of making the young Tinker highly superstitious, so that he appears to have thought simply attending church twice a Sabbath was enough for his soul. Yet, the authors of these works, Arthur Dent and Lewis Bayly, spoke to the Tinker, while still a sinful wretch, in a way that few others had been able to. It is, then, perhaps no surprise that the writings of other saints of the past would have a profound impact upon the man.

John had spent a great deal of time reflecting on Scripture, and various texts had flooded his soul with immeasurable peace and joy. It is true that, for a time, he began to think of himself as existing beyond all hope of forgiveness, writing, 'And now I was sorry that God had made me man, for I feared I was a reprobate,'[53] but Scripture was always the main tool that the Lord used to lift Bunyan up and out of the miry clay. For, on one occasion, Bunyan heard a sermon preached on Song of Songs 4:1, which states, 'Behold, thou art fair, my love, behold, thou art fair...' He explained, in *Grace Abounding*, how the pastor made the two words 'my love' the chief subject of the sermon, saying, 'If it be so, that the saved soul is Christ's love, when under temptation and desertion; then poor tempted soul, when thou art assaulted, and afflicted with temptations, and the hidings of God's face, yet think on these two words, "My love," still.'[54]

Reflecting on those words on the way home, 'These words began thus to kindle in my spirit, Thou art My Love, thou art My Dove, twenty times together; and still as they ran in my mind, they waxed stronger and warmer, and began to make me look up.'[55] It was moments like these, of genuine reflection upon the Word of God, that continually brought him closer to Christ and the assurance of salvation that he so desperately sought.

This is not to say that it was merely an uphill climb at this time. There were moments where, after having been

---

53. Ibid., 16.
54. Ibid., 16-17.
55. Ibid., 17.

on the ascent for some time, John would come plummeting back down. He recalled how, at one point, he began thinking blasphemous thoughts and asking questions like, 'As, whether there were in truth, a God or Christ? And whether the holy scriptures were not rather a fable, and cunning story, than the holy and pure word of God?'[56]

Even those moments wherein Bunyan lighted upon the great truths of the gospel were often overshadowed by the great temptations that would then weigh down upon his soul. It was as though every time he drew near to the truth of salvation and assurance in Jesus Christ alone, Satan was there and ready to hurl his fiery darts at the Tinker. There were moments when he believed himself to be possessed of a devil; on other occasions, he lamented that he could not shed tears over sin in the same way as others or memorize God's Word as others did so well.[57] It was as though every time God pulled Bunyan just a little bit closer to himself, Satan was clinging onto his arm, pulling him back in the other direction. It was like the tormenting dreams of his childhood were now playing out in his life. Now, it was no longer imagined devils attempting to drag him down to hell in nightmares, but the actual devil waging war over his soul. Recalling an occasion like this, Bunyan recorded how it was like the devil was saying to him:

> You are very hot for mercy, but I will cool you; this frame shall not last always: many have been as hot as you for a spurt, but I have quenched their zeal (and with this, such and such, who were fallen off, would be set before mine eyes). Then I should be afraid that I should do so too: But, thought I, I am glad this comes into my mind: well, I will watch, and take what care I can. Though you do, said Satan, I shall be too hard for you; I will cool you insensibly, by degrees, by little and little. What care I, saith he, though I be seven years in chilling your heart, if I can do it at last? Continual rocking will lull a crying child asleep: I will ply it close, but I will have my end accomplished.

---

56. Ibid., 1:17.
57. See: Ibid., 18.

Though you be burning hot at present, I can pull you from this fire; I shall have you cold before it be long.[58]

Yet, even in these moments, God did not let go. Sermons, meditation on Scripture, and other graces were afforded to Bunyan to refresh his weary soul when he most needed it. Alas, how often the children of God find the deep springs of Scripture most refreshing when they have spent time in the wilderness of temptation and affliction!

Scripture like, 'For he hath made him to be sin for us, who knew no sin; that we might be made the righteousness of God in him,' (2 Cor. 5:21) refreshed him with its sweet promise. When, on another occasion, he asked, 'What ground have I to say that, who have been so vile and abominable, should ever inherit eternal life?' The answer came from the Scriptures, 'What shall we say to these things? If God be for us, who can be against us? Rom. viii.31. That also was an help unto me, Because I live, ye shall live also. John xiv.19.'[59]

What the Tinker really needed during this time was a pastor who could guide him into the truth of the Scriptures; a pastor who could act as a physician for his soul. This he would find in the person of John Gifford. A Kentish man, his life was an interesting one. According to George Offor, he was a Royalist soldier in the English Civil War who was supposed to be hung for some crimes he had committed. However, he had managed to escape and eventually made his way to Bedford. What made him so approachable to Bunyan was his own troubled past. Offor explains that Gifford had been, 'Addicted to swearing, drinking, and gambling, he, in distress at a serious loss, vowed repentance; he became greatly distressed under conviction of sin; at length his mind was enlightened, the Holy Spirit led him to forgiveness by the atonement of Christ, and his heart was filled with a hitherto unknown source of blessedness.'[60]

Having experienced the blessed peace of conversion, Gifford began a church in 1650, and Bunyan joined it in 1653. The two were close companions, and it is not to be doubted that their relatively brief time together was very fruitful for

58. Ibid., 19.
59. Ibid.
60. Ibid., 19.

the Tinker. Later, in the preface to Bunyan's 1658 work *A Few Sighs from Hell*, Gifford wrote kindly of the Tinker.[61] 'I have to say, that I verily believe God hath counted him faithful, and put him in to the ministry; and though his outward condition and former employment was mean, and his human learning small yet is he one that hath acquaintance with God, and taught by his Spirit, and hath been used in his hand to do souls good.'[62] These are warm and kind words, filled with grace and are, perhaps, some of the best that any could hope to have written of them. It is fair, then, to say that Gifford and Bunyan were close. In fact, though incredibly early in Bunyan's public ministry of preaching and teaching, Gifford would go on to say that many had already felt the power of Bunyan's words and he was sure that, if God would permit, his words would reach countless more still.

Gifford was vital in helping Bunyan to find assurance of salvation. Bunyan explains his manner of ministry by noting that, 'At this time also I sat under the ministry of holy Mr. Gifford, whose doctrine, by God's grace, was much for my stability.'[63] His greatest help to Bunyan came in his teaching the Tinker that our salvation is found in Christ alone, and not in much striving or working. Bunyan explained:

> This man made it much his business to deliver the people of God from all those false and unsound tests, that by nature we are prone to. He would bid us take special heed, that we took not up any truth upon trust; as from this, or that, or any other man or men; but to cry mightily to God, that He would convince us of the reality thereof, and set us down therein by His own Spirit in the holy word; For, said he, if you do otherwise, when temptations come, if strongly, you not having received them with evidence from heaven, will find you want that help and strength now to resist, that once you thought you had.[64]

---

61. Though Gifford had already passed away by 1656, he evidently completed the preface to Bunyan's 1658 publication before his own death.

62. John Gifford, In the Preface to John Bunyan, *A Few Sighs from Hell, Works*, 3:672.

63. Bunyan, *Grace Abounding to the Chief of Sinners, Works*, 1:20.

64. Ibid.

Now, as helpful as Gifford was, the Tinker had spent some time yearning for help in truly defeating his temptations. His earnest desire was to find a saint from the past who would write to him with deep and perfect clarity regarding the things of God. Likely it was his acquaintance with the books of his first wife that created this longing within him. He longed to understand the nature of Law and Grace from one who had gone before him. Around this time, Bunyan was granted a copy of Martin Luther's *Commentary on Galatians*. He does not say from whence it came, but it is possible he attained a copy from Gifford or someone else in Bedford. Of Luther's writing, the Tinker explains:

> After many such longings in my mind, the God, in Whose hands are all our days and ways, did cast into my hand (one day) a book of Martin Luther's; it was his Comment on the Galatians; it also was so old, that it was ready to fall piece from piece if I did but turn it over. Now I was pleased much that such an old book had fallen into my hand, the which when I had but a little way perused, I found my condition in his experience so largely and profoundly handled, as if his book had been written out of my heart. This made me marvel: for thus thought I, This man could not know any thing of the state of Christians now, but must needs write and speak the experience of former days.[65]

Luther's writing had an undeniably large impact on Bunyan. He would go on to say, 'I do prefer this book of Martin Luther upon the Galatians (excepting the Holy Bible) before all the books that ever I had seen, as most fit for a wounded conscience.'[66] Within this work, wherein Luther wrote of the distinction between Law and Gospel, Grace and Works, Bunyan found a kindred spirit who, like himself and Gifford, had been crushed beneath the weight of the Law. Herein Bunyan learned the gospel truths that salvation is found through faith alone, in Christ alone, by God's grace alone, according to the Scriptures alone, all to the glory of God alone.

Here, Bunyan's soul was kindled with fire from above, and he found a passionate love for Christ that he had not yet known. He wrote, 'And now I found, as I thought, that I loved

---

65. Ibid., 22.
66. Ibid.

Christ dearly: Oh! methought my soul cleaved unto Him, my affections cleaved unto Him; I felt love to Him as hot as fire; and now, as Job said, I thought I should die in my nest...'[67]

How glorious the newfound love for Christ within the newborn child of God!

But, alas, such a love as this was soon to be tried.

Continued Temptations of the Saint

Bunyan had truly believed in Christ by the grace of God and experienced the blessed peace that comes from knowing the Lord and being known by Him. But the temptations were far from over. Let the one who believes himself to have attained perfection learn well from Bunyan's own experience.

After lighting upon the truth of the gospel, and after the Tinker had only just written, 'I loved Christ dearly: Oh! methought my soul cleaved unto Him, my affections cleaved unto Him; I felt love to Him as hot as fire...', [68] the temptations came with a vengeance. Yet, what a passionate declaration of faith this had been! John felt, with assurance and certainty, that he had been joined together to Christ by faith and would never let go of this lovely Savior. In this moment, he would have eagerly declared, 'I am my beloved's, and my beloved is mine' (Song 6:3).

Such faith in Christ is wonderful, beautiful, and greatly to be desired. But the danger of such faith is that it may, if the child of God is not careful, produce a pride which sees itself as above temptation. This is why the Scripture warns, 'Wherefore let him that thinketh he standeth take heed lest he fall' (1 Cor. 10:12). As Bunyan would soon find, the reason the Christian is commanded to put on the full armor of God is because the temptations toward the one who has been saved do not depart. In some seasons, temptations can grow all the more severe for the Christian.

Bunyan recalled that soon after he had experienced such great assurance that, 'I did quickly find, that my great love was but little; and that I, who had, as I thought, such burning love to Jesus Christ, could let Him go again for a very trifle,—

---

67. Ibid.
68. Ibid.

God can tell how to abase us, and can hide pride from man. Quickly after this my love was tried to purpose.'[69]

One of the most serious temptations to come during this time was one in which Bunyan felt himself tempted by Satan to sell Christ in exchange for the riches of the world. Again and again, Bunyan would hear the tempting words in his mind, 'Sell him, sell him, sell him, sell him...' And again and again, Bunyan would refuse. Until, one day, having been exhausted by constant temptations while working, eating, and lying in bed—indeed, every waking moment—the Tinker finally proclaimed, 'Let Him go, if He will!'[70]

This began a long and troublesome period where Bunyan could not help but wonder if he had made shipwreck of his faith. Yet, believing the doctrine of election and perseverance to be true, he trusted in the sovereignty of God to keep him forever in His mighty grasp (John 10:28-30). Wrestling against this, though, was the concern that he was no different from a Judas—one who made a visible and outward confession, but inwardly, was a traitor.

Bunyan noted this conflict when he wrote:

> Now I saw, that as God had His hand in all the providences and dispensations that overtook His elect; so He had His hand in all the temptations that they had to sin against Him; not to animate them to wickedness, but to choose their temptations and troubles for them; and also to leave them for a time, to such sins only that might not destroy, but humble them; as might not put them beyond, but lay them in the way of the renewing His mercy... As all things wrought together for the best, and to do good to them that were the called, according to His purpose, so I thought that all things wrought for my damage, and for my eternal overthrow.[71]

This was a time of deep anguish and sorrow. But it would not last forever. Though he continued with this affliction of the soul for some time, he finally lighted upon the truth that, 'for the word of the law and wrath, must give place to the word of life and grace; because, though the word of condemnation

---

69. Ibid.
70. Ibid., 23.
71. Ibid., 25.

be glorious, yet the word of life and salvation doth far exceed in glory.'[72]

What would it take for the Tinker to finally kill these besetting sins of doubt, lay aside the snares of temptation, and embrace the free offer of the gospel as being truly free and truly for him? As the Lord would have it, a walk through a field and meditation upon Scripture was just the prescription needed for Bunyan's poor soul.

The following portion of his writing is striking for its profundity and beauty in describing the assurance of salvation wrought suddenly within his soul. He wrote:

> But one day, as I was passing in the field, and that too with some dashes on my conscience, fearing lest yet all was not right, suddenly this sentence fell upon my soul, Thy righteousness is in heaven; and methought withal, I saw with the eyes of my soul, Jesus Christ at God's right hand: there, I say, was my righteousness; so that wherever I was, or whatever I was doing, God could not say of me, He wants My righteousness; for that was just before Him. I also saw moreover, that it was not my good frame of heart that made my righteousness better, nor yet my bad frame that made my righteousness worse; for my righteousness was Jesus Christ Himself, The same yesterday, to-day, and for ever. Heb. xiii.8.
>
> Now did my chains fall off my legs indeed; I was loosed from my afflictions and irons; my temptations also fled away; so that from that time those dreadful scriptures of God left off to trouble me: now went I also home rejoicing, for the grace and love of God; so when I came home, I looked to see if I could find that sentence; Thy righteousness is in heaven, but could not find such a saying; wherefore my heart began to sink again, only that was brought to my remembrance, 1 Cor. i.30, Christ Jesus, who of God is made unto us wisdom, and righteousness, and sanctification, and redemption; by this word I saw the other sentence true.
>
> For by this scripture I saw that the Man Christ Jesus, as He is distinct from us, as touching His bodily presence, so He is our righteousness and sanctification before God. Here therefore I lived, for some time, very sweetly at peace with God through

---

72. Ibid., 22

Christ; Oh! methought, Christ! Christ! there was nothing but Christ that was before my eyes: I was not now (only) for looking upon this and the other benefits of Christ apart, as of His blood, burial, or resurrection, but considering Him as a whole Christ! as He in whom all these, and all His other virtues, relations, offices and operations met together, and that He sat on the right hand of God in heaven.

'Twas glorious to me to see His exaltation, and the worth and prevalency of all His benefits, and that because now I could look from myself to Him and should reckon, that all those graces of God that now were green on me, were yet but like those cracked groats and fourpence-halfpennies that rich men carry in their purses, when their gold is in their trunks at home: Oh! I saw my gold was in my trunk at home! In Christ my Lord and Saviour. Now Christ was all; all my wisdom, all my righteousness, all my sanctification, and all my redemption.

Further, the Lord did also lead me into the mystery of union with the Son of God; that I was joined to Him, that I was flesh of His flesh, and bone of His bone; and now was that word sweet to me in Eph. v.30. By this also was my faith in Him, as my righteousness, the more confirmed in me; for if He and I were one, then His righteousness was mine, His merits mine, His victory also mine. Now could I see myself in heaven and earth at once: in heaven by my Christ, by my head, by my righteousness and life, though on earth by my body or person.[73]

The Lord Finishes What He Has Begun

It took a long time for the full benefits of conversion to take root in the deep recesses of Bunyan's soul, but finally Bunyan knew that Christ was all his righteousness. Finally, the Tinker understood that, through faith, he was united to Christ, and union with Christ means the child of God experiences the full benefits and blessings of the Savior. John now knew that Christ's merits are the saint's merits through faith; His victory is the saint's victory through faith; all that is Christ's is the saint's through faith. Finally, Bunyan would have been able to sing, with great joy, John Newton's hymn 'Amazing Grace.' Had he heard the song, he would have personally identified

---

73. Ibid., 1:35-36.

himself with the miserable wretch who once was blind, but now saw, and who was lost, but now was found by Christ.

It was this deep knowledge of his own sin, and the great grace of God, that led him to be a genuine soul winner for Christ. As he wrote in *The Jerusalem Sinner Saved*:

> I speak by experience. I was one of these lousy ones, one of these great sin-breeders; I infected all the youth of the town where I was born, with all manner of youthful vanities. The neighbours counted me so; my practice proved me so: wherefore Christ Jesus took me first; and taking me first, the contagion was much allayed all the town over. When God made me sigh, they would hearken, and inquiringly say, What's the matter with John? They also gave their various opinions of me; but, as I said, sin cooled, and failed, as to his full career. When I went out to seek the bread of life, some of them would follow, and the rest be put into a muse at home. Yea, almost the town, at first, at times would go out to hear at the place where I found good; yea, young and old for a while had some reformation on them; also some of them, perceiving that God had mercy upon me, came crying to him for mercy too.[74]

Bunyan beautifully saw God's grace upon his life as an amazingly powerful act of the Lord whereby others could be drawn to Christ. The Tinker would never again glory in his sin, but he would utilize the change that God had wrought upon him and his former life of sin in order to reach his old friends and companions. In fact, he would regularly preach and write of how, if God's grace had abounded toward him, the chief of all sinners, then it was of certainty that God's grace was sufficient to save all others who would draw near to Christ by faith.

Not only was God's grace sufficient to save, though. Bunyan also knew God's grace was extraordinary enough to *keep* saved and even *complete* the work of salvation. The Tinker knew that God's golden chain of salvation in Romans 8:29-30 was absolutely true: 'For whom he did foreknow, he also did predestinate to be conformed to the image of his Son, that he might be the firstborn among many brethren. Moreover whom he did predestinate, them he also called: and whom he

---

called, them he also justified: and whom he justified, them he also glorified.'

The Apostle Paul, writing to the church at Philippi, offered an amazing comfort to troubled saints when he wrote that he was, 'Being confident of this very thing, that he which hath begun a good work in you will perform it until the day of Jesus Christ' (Phil. 1:6). Many, who do not quite understand the nature of salvation, have a pervasive fear that they could somehow mess things up so badly so that the Lord would finally cast them away and turn His back on them. Bunyan's story proves just the opposite. Not only will the Lord save those whom He intends to save through election, but He will preserve those whom He saves through the definite atonement of the Son.

Even when we find ourselves riddled with temptation and grieved by sin, we must remember that our Savior's atonement is perfectly sufficient to wash away our sins, past, present, and future. On other occasions, His love can even constrain us from committing great and heinous sins (2 Cor. 5:14). As Bunyan himself noted:

> As, first, sometimes, I have been so loaden with my sins, that I could not tell where to rest, nor what to do; yea, at such times I thought it would have taken away my senses; yet at that time God through grace hath all of a sudden so effectually applied the blood that was spilt at Mount Calvary out of the side of Jesus, unto my poor, wounded, guilty conscience, that presently I have found such a sweet, solid, sober, heart-comforting peace, that it hath made me as if it [my terror] had not been, and withal the same, I may say, and I ought to say, the power of it, hath had such a powerful operation upon my soul, that I have for a time been in a strait and trouble to think that I should love and honour Him no more, the virtue of His blood hath so constrained me.[75]

We have spent a great deal of time searching Bunyan's conversion experience, but we have done so for two very important purposes: Firstly, so that we would remember that Bunyan, like us, was a sinner saved by grace alone. There was nothing in him that was lovely, or admirable, or of worthiness

---

75. Bunyan, *The Law and Grace Unfolded*, *Works*, 1:549.

before Christ imparted the blessing of salvation to him. Let the reader understand: If Bunyan could be saved by God's grace; if the Apostle Paul could be saved by God's grace; if *I* could be saved by God's grace; then so too can all others, for God's grace abounds to even the chief of sinners.

Secondly, let Bunyan serve as an example that temptations and besetting sins are common within the Christian's experience, but must still be put to death. Striving, struggling, and fighting against sin may, at times, seem impossible. But, remember the truth Bunyan learned: We who are united to Christ by faith will persevere in the faith because Christ's righteousness, merits, and victory are all ours according to the infinite grace of God, which is far greater than all our sins.

CHAPTER 4

The Shepherd Called to the Field of His Flock: Bunyan's Calling to Ministry

Now I saw, upon a time, when he was walking in the fields, that he was (as he was wont) reading in his book, and greatly distressed in his mind; and as he read, he burst out, as he had done before, crying, 'What shall I do to be saved?' Acts xvi.30, 31.

I saw also that he looked this way, and that way, as if he would run; yet he stood still because (as I perceived) he could not tell which way to go. I looked then, and saw a man named Evangelist coming to him, and he asked, 'Wherefore dost thou cry?'

He answered, 'Sir, I perceive, by the book in my hand, that I am condemned to die, and after that to come to judgment, He. ix.27; and I find that I am not willing (Job xvi.21, 22) to do the first, nor able (Eze. xxii.14) to do the second.'

Then said Evangelist, 'Why not willing to die, since this life is attended with so many evils?' The man answered, 'Because, I fear that this burden that is upon my back will sink me lower than the grave, and I shall fall into Tophet. Is. xxx.33. And Sir, if I be not fit to go to prison, I am not fit

to go to judgment, and from thence to execution; and the
thoughts of these things make me cry.'

Then said Evangelist, 'If this be thy condition, why standest
thou still?' He answered, 'Because I know not whither to go.'
Then he gave him a parchment roll, and there was written
within, 'Fly from the wrath to come.' Matt. iii.7.

The man therefore read it, and looking upon Evangelist very
carefully, said, 'Whither must I fly?' Then said Evangelist,
(pointing with his finger over a very wide field,) 'Do you
see yonder wicket-gate?' Matt. vii.13, 14. The man said, 'No.'
Then said the other, 'Do you see yonder shining light?'
Ps. cxix.105; 2 Pe. i.19. He said, 'I think I do.' Then said
Evangelist, 'Keep that light in your eye, and go up directly
thereto, so shalt thou see the gate; at which, when thou
knockest, it shall be told thee what thou shalt do.' So I saw
in my dream that the man began to run. Now he had not
run far from his own door when his wife and children,
perceiving it, began to cry after him to return; but the man
put his fingers in his ears, and ran on crying, Life! life!
eternal life! Lu. xiv.26. So he looked not behind him,
Ge. xix.17, but fled towards the middle of the plain.

(Evangelist preaches to Christian in *The Pilgrim's Progress*)

Show me a man who has gotten his theology solely through
education and show me a man who has learned the great truth
of God's Word through a relationship with Christ and diligent
study of the Scriptures, and the difference between the two
will be as plain as night and day. While this is not to say
that seminary education is without merit (there is great value
in training under those men who possess great wisdom and
knowledge of the Scriptures), nor is this to say that training is
unimportant (every single pastor ought to give himself fully
over to prayer and the study of God's Word, as the Apostles
were devoted to prayer and the ministry of the Word in Acts
6:4), it is to say that there is a large difference between those
who simply know some truths about the Lord and His Word
and those who actually *know* the Lord and the truth of His

Word. When both learning and experience come together, the Apostle Pauls of this world are born. But it takes Peters to move mountains, and Bunyan belonged to this latter category. He may have lacked the nuanced training of a contemporary like John Owen, but he was as spiritually gifted as any one of his contemporaries, for what he lacked in education, he more than made up for in experience and heartfelt gratitude toward the God who had saved him.

In this chapter, we will trace John's call into the ministry. We will examine how he came to be a writer and preacher and attempt to understand how God had particularly prepared him for this special calling over his life. We will not, however, trace his ministry very far in this chapter, for, in the next chapter, we will see how persecution struck the Puritans, and the Bunyans in particular.

Prepared by Grace

Hindsight is twenty-twenty, as they say, and Bunyan proves this to be true. Looking back over the long years and days of besetting sins, terrible temptations, awful doubting, and complete lack of assurance, the Tinker finally recognized what the problem had been. His eyes were not set upon Christ, and he had neglected to approach the throne of God's grace to obtain mercy and find grace to help him in his time of need and battle against sin and temptation (Heb. 4:16). He wrote:

> This I had not done, and therefore was thus suffered to sin and fall, according to what is written, Pray that ye enter not into temptation. And truly this very thing is to this day of such weight and awe upon me, that I dare not, when I come before the Lord, go of my knees, until I intreat Him for help and mercy against the temptations that are to come; and I do beseech thee, reader, that thou learn to beware of my negligence, by the afflictions, that for this thing I did for days, and months, and years, with sorrow undergo.[1]

Some learn best through the school of hard knocks and this seems to have been Bunyan's own experience. It was not that the Lord despised him or had rejected him but that the Lord

---

1. John Bunyan, *Grace Abounding to the Chief of Sinners*, *Works*, 1:37.

had set His love upon the Tinker and would, through the difficulties experienced, teach him to cling to Christ and His promises with greater passion and love than he would if he had simply never experienced the many trials he did on his journey.

Joseph, in Genesis, was sold into slavery not because God had abandoned him, but because God loved him and planned to use him and his misfortune to save his family during the famine. Job was not tempted by Satan because God despised him, but because God loved him and knew that Job would put the devil to open shame. Jesus was not forsaken at the Cross because the Father was looking for a reason to abandon His Son, but so that rather, through His death, burial, and resurrection, God could then save sinners. Through the death of the Son, the anguished cries of 'My God, my God, why hast thou forsaken me?' have given way to the promise of, 'My child, my child, I will never leave nor forsake you.'

God is able to take situations that seem hopeless and helpless and turn them around for the good of His saints and His greatest glory. As Paul wrote in Romans 8:28, 'And we know that all things work together for good to them that love God, to them who are the called according to his purpose.' Bunyan's life serves as a testament to the wisdom of God's sovereign ordination over our lives.

Looking back on why he had suffered so many terrible temptations and doubts, Bunyan saw a number of reasons for why God had permitted and allowed them. Later in his life, he saw them as acts of God's grace, whereby he was taught greater trust and assurance that would help him, not only in his own walk with Christ, but in his ability to counsel those who struggled through the same storms that he had.

In *Grace Abounding*, Bunyan notes that the first great benefit of the temptations he had experienced was that he learned to hold the blessing and glory of the Triune God continually before his eyes:

> I was made continually to possess in my soul a very wonderful sense both of the blessing and glory of God, and of His beloved Son; in the temptation that went before, my soul was perplexed with unbelief, blasphemy, hardness of heart, questions about

the being of God, Christ, the truth of the word, and certainty of the world to come: I say, then I was greatly assaulted and tormented with atheism, but now the case was otherwise; now was God and Christ continually before my face, though not in a way of comfort, but in a way of exceeding dread and terror. The glory of the holiness of God, did at this time break me to pieces; and the bowels and compassion of Christ did break me as on the wheel; for I could not consider Him but as a lost and rejected Christ, the remembrance of which, was as the continual breaking of my bones.[2]

Secondly, he received the benefit of truly learning to love the Scriptures. As we saw in the previous chapter, it took him an exceptionally long time to come to a point where he was assured that he possessed a true salvation in Christ. But during those years of inner struggles and spiritual turmoil, the Scriptures were continually before his eyes and meditation on them was a regular part of his life. He wrote:

The scriptures also were wonderful things unto me; I saw that the truth and verity of them were the keys of the kingdom of heaven; those that the scriptures favour, they must inherit bliss; but those that they oppose and condemn, must perish for evermore: Oh! this word, For the scriptures cannot be broken, would rend the caul [covering] of my heart: and so would that other, Whose sins ye remit, they are remitted; but whose sins ye retain, they are retained. Now I saw the apostles to be the elders of the city of refuge. Joshua xx.4. Those that they were to receive in, were received to life; but those that they shut out, were to be slain by the avenger of blood...

I was made to see more into the nature of the promises than ever I was before; for I lying now trembling under the mighty hand of God, continually torn and rent by the thundering of His justice: this made me with careful heart, and watchful eye, with great fearfulness to turn over every leaf, and with much diligence, mixed with trembling, to consider every sentence, together with its natural force and latitude.[3]

Thirdly, Bunyan learned to truly latch on to the promises of God, not as some distant promises made to people who

---

2. Ibid., 37.
3. Ibid., 37-38.

were yet far off, but as promises made directly to himself. He understood, now, 'And if ye be Christ's, then are ye Abraham's seed, and heirs according to the promise' (Gal. 3:29). As he wrote:

> I was greatly holden off from my former foolish practice of putting by the word of promise when saw it came into my mind; for now, though I could not suck that comfort and sweetness from the promise, as I had done at other times; yet, like to a man sinking, I would catch at all I saw: formerly I thought I might not meddle with the promise, unless I felt its comfort, but now 'twas no time thus to do; the avenger of blood too hardly did pursue me.
>
> Now therefore I was glad to catch at that word which yet I feared I had no ground or right to own; and even to leap into the bosom of that promise that yet I feared did shut its heart against me. Now also I should labour to take the word as God hath laid it down, without restraining the natural force of one syllable thereof: O! what did I now see in that blessed sixth of John: And him that cometh to me, I will in no wise cast out. John vi.37. Now I began to consider with myself, that God hath a bigger mouth to speak with, than I had a heart to conceive with; I thought also with myself, that He spake not His words in haste, or in an unadvised heat, but with infinite wisdom and judgment, and in very truth and faithfulness. 2 Sam. iii.28.[4]

How great a truth the Tinker expressed! 'God hath a bigger mouth to speak with, than I had a heart to conceive with.' The truth was that the Holy Spirit had prompted John to come to Jesus, and Jesus would not now cast him out. The promise was simply that: A promise that Jesus would not cast out. Bunyan could now settle himself in that promise, knowing this was made by a God who spoke with 'infinite wisdom and judgment, and in very truth and faithfulness.'

Fourthly, Bunyan learned through his temptations of the greatness of God. 'I never saw those heights and depths in grace, and love, and mercy, as I saw after this temptation; great sins to draw out great grace; and where guilt is most terrible and fierce, there the mercy of God in Christ, when showed

---

4. Ibid., 38.

to the soul, appears most high and mighty.'[5] He learned that 'where sin abounded, grace did much more abound' (Rom. 5:20) and the great hope and assurance of every Christian is that Christ, by great grace, saves great sinners. He remembered how:

> I had two or three times, at or about my deliverance from this temptation, such strange apprehensions of the grace of God, that I could hardly bear up under it: it was so out of measure amazing, when I thought it could reach me, that I do think if that sense of it had abode long upon me, it would have made me incapable for business.[6]

Surely, this is only scratching the surface of what Bunyan had learned during the long course of his temptations and doubting. What cannot be doubted is that, during this period, the Lord had been preparing Bunyan for the peculiar task of ministry that was set before him. After all, who better to minister the grace of God to the wretched and depraved and suffering, than one who was once a depraved and suffering wretch who had experienced the great grace of God?

Part of what made Bunyan so fit to be both a preacher and writer was that he understood what many of his listeners and readers struggled with themselves. He knew what it was to be deep in sin. He also knew the horrors of possessing a hardened heart and seared conscience. He could also relate to those whose consciences were so wounded by the Word of God and judgment of His wrath that they knew not what to do. He knew the sweetness of finally embracing the promises of God after a long wrestling match with the Lord. He knew, firsthand, the comfort of embracing the Savior who had embraced him.

It took him a very long time to grasp the fact that it is Jesus who saves sinners, and not trying, working, or striving. But once the truth was grasped, the Tinker understood, as though God Himself had said it directly to him:

> I was as if I had heard it thus expounded to me: Sinner, thou thinkest, that because thy sins and infirmities, I cannot save

---

5. Ibid.
6. Ibid.

thy soul; but behold My Son is by me, and upon Him I look, and not on thee, and shall deal with thee according as I am pleased with Him. At this I was greatly lightened in my mind, and made to understand, that God could justify a sinner at any time; it was but His looking upon Christ, and imputing His benefits to us, and the work was forthwith done.[7]

This was the message, now fully grasped and understood and delighted in, that Bunyan would now be compelled to take to Bedford and, indeed, the world.

The Outward Call Given

Most Christians distinguish between callings of God over the life of the one who is called into ministry to teach, preach, and publicly proclaim the Word of God. The callings do not always occur at the same time, and certain ministers of the Word may experience the two callings at different times. However, it seems to more often be the case that the first calling received is that which is labeled the 'outward calling.' This is where others will recognize that God has equipped and gifted the saint in a number of special ways that makes them a most likely candidate for minister of the Word. After this, if the man in question has truly been called into gospel ministry, he will receive the assurance of an 'inward call,' wherein the Holy Spirit within him will affirm the truth of that outward call that has been received.

This is similar, in many ways, to the gospel call. Typically, the sinner hears the 'outward call' as the gospel message is proclaimed and the sinner commanded to 'Repent, and believe in Christ and His death, burial, and resurrection!' Then, after the outward calling is given, an 'inward calling' takes place as the Holy Spirit pierces the sinner's hardened heart with the harpooning spear of God's glorious grace. Then, through this inward call, the sinner is drawn, sweetly and tenderly, to the eternal embrace of Christ.

Bunyan's experience was much like this in both cases. When it came to his call to ministry, others recognized in him, after he had been walking with the Lord for about six

---

7. Ibid., 39.

years, a special dispensation of the grace of God that would enable him to minister the Word of God in a special way that few others could. He recorded how:

> After I had been about five or six years awakened, and helped myself to see both the want and worth of Jesus Christ our Lord, and also enabled to venture my soul upon Him; some of the most able among the saints with us, I say, the most able for judgment and holiness of life, as they conceived, did perceive that God had counted me worth to understand something of His will in His holy and blessed word, and had given me utterance in some measure, to express what I saw to others, for edification; therefore they desired me, and that with much earnestness, that I would be willing, at sometimes to take in hand, in one of the meetings, to speak a word of exhortation unto them.[8]

These saints of the Bedford Free Church, where Gifford pastored, ought to be commended for recognizing in the Tinker the gift of preaching and teaching, without being respecters of persons. How easily may the congregation of Bedford have looked to poor Bunyan and said, 'He is poor, untrained, unscholarly, and far from the type of man we would want to enter the pastorate, or preach publicly for the Word of God.' Instead, they looked at him in his intellectual weaknesses and frailties and said, 'You, sir, have been equipped by God's grace in a special and peculiar way to be one who expounds the Word of God!' The congregation at Bedford was most encouraging in this manner.

Again, it should be noted that Bunyan's ability to minister the Word of God came entirely as a gifting of the Holy Spirit. Only a few years prior, the young Tinker had been given to all manner of wretched lasciviousness, but now he had become a devout follower of Christ. Such a drastic change, in such a short span of time, can only be explained by the inner workings of God's great grace. Likewise, his ability to remember, quote, and exposit the Scriptures can also only be attributed to God's great grace. This was a man who, in his own words, had almost all but forgotten the meager education he had received as a child. He had almost all but forgotten

---

8. Ibid., 40-41.

how to even read and write.[9] That this man then read—and strenuously studied!—the Scriptures is one thing to marvel at, but even greater marvel still is that he wrote nearly sixty works of Christian literature!

George Offor explained that Bunyan's calling into ministry was typically how dissenting ministers were often called. He explained:

> First, their gifts in prayer and conversation upon Divine things, and aptness in illustrating and confirming what they advance from the Scriptures, is noticed; and, secondly, they are encouraged to pray with and address the poor children in a Sunday School. If they manifest an aptness to teach, they are, thirdly, invited to give an exhortation to the church privately; and then, fourthly, they are encouraged to pray and preach among the poor in country villages and in workhouses.[10]

This historical insight is helpful in explaining the process that Bunyan underwent. The congregation he had joined at Bedford was, in fact, filled with dissenters, but there was still an order to the way things were to be done. Effectively, they were congregationalists in practice, but not just anyone could be called to the ministry, and not just anyone could be entrusted with the all-important task of preaching and teaching the Word of God—the very Bread of Life—to those who hungered and thirsted after righteousness. The man called to such a task had to be fit to perform the duties thereof.

So it was that Bunyan was asked to preach for them, privately, and he struggled with the very thought of even considering doing so! Seldom does a minister run to the pulpit when the outward call is given. It is said that, when John Knox had been asked to preach by his own church, he ran from them, wept, and locked himself away. John Calvin had to practically be forced into Geneva to preach the Word of God. For Bunyan, it was the simple and continuing entreating of the Bedford congregation that led him to finally acquiesce to them and do as they requested.

---

9. Ibid., 6.

10. Offor, *Grace Abounding to the Chief of Sinners, Works*, 1:41.

He preached twice to the Bedford assembly. He humbly recorded how, in these two meetings, he did, 'Though with much weakness and infirmity, discover my gift amongst them; at which they not only seemed to be, but did solemnly protest, as in the sight of the great God, they were both affected and comforted; and gave thanks to the Father of mercies, for the grace bestowed on me.'[11] Bunyan had more than passed the congregational test; he had surpassed expectations. The people who heard these sermons experienced the comfort of the Holy Spirit that is only attended by the right handling of God's Word and proper division of truth (2 Tim. 2:15). They praised God because they recognized what others would soon see as well: Bunyan had a great working of God's grace bestowed upon him, and God was going to use the Tinker to accomplish His mighty purposes on earth.

It is seldom the case, however, that a minister runs to or embraces his calling full sail on the first occasion of outward confirmation. Consider how men like John Calvin and John Knox initially desired to flee from their callings. Even Jonah did not desire to preach in Nineveh. Yet, the Lord always gets his men. Bunyan would accompany members of his church as they went out to teach in the countryside of Bedford, but he would remain private with his giftings. When opportunities presented themselves, and he could do so in relative obscurity, he would sometimes feel compelled to share the truth of God's Word with those they had gone to minister to. All this time, however, he purposefully avoided the spotlight. His was not a personality given to the seeking of attention. He much preferred to remain unknown and obscure before men.

The Bedford church greatly desired Bunyan to accept the calling of becoming a regular public preacher of the Word of God, but the Tinker struggled with the calling. Could one such as he really be called to become a minister of the Word of God? One text in particular helped him during this time: 'I beseech you, brethren, (ye know the house of Stephanas, that it is the firstfruits of Achaia, and that they have addicted themselves to the ministry of the saints,) That ye submit yourselves unto such, and to every one that helpeth with us, and laboureth'

---

11. Bunyan, *Grace Abounding to the Chief of Sinners*, *Works*, 1:41.

(1 Cor. 16:15-16). Through this text, Bunyan began to realize that God equips and gifts the saints with particular abilities not so that they will run and hide and bury them, but so that they will use them for the betterment of the church and the edification of the saints of God. He realized that, if God had truly gifted him to preach the Word of God, then he had no choice but to preach the Word of God. Thus, he wrote:

> Wherefore, though of myself of all the saints the most unworthy; yet I, but with great fear and trembling at the sight of my own weakness, did set upon the work, and did according to my gift, and the proportion of my faith, preach that blessed gospel that God had showed me in the holy word of truth: which when the country understood, they came in to hear the word by hundreds, and that from all parts, though upon sundry and divers accounts.[12]

Let it not be lost on the reader that, when Bunyan finally embraced his calling to preach the Word of God, hundreds came from all around to hear his preaching. Whereas there are some saints, like George Whitefield and Charles Spurgeon, who are fondly remembered for their ability to preach with exceptional ability, Bunyan is often just remembered as a writer of allegories. What an injustice this does to the memory of the man! There was something about his preaching that gripped his hearers and led them to travel to hear him preach from all around.

Some, especially this early in their walk with Christ, may have grown conceited and puffed up with pride. But not Bunyan. He knew the pitfalls of pride well. Rather than puffing him up, the crowds moved him to pity. He saw the people as Jesus once saw the throngs of humanity rushing to meet Him: As sheep without a shepherd, and as dying men seeking a Savior. Bunyan thanked the Lord that:

> He gave unto me some measure of bowels and pity for their souls, which also did put me forward to labour, with great diligence and earnestness, to find out such a word as might, if God would bless, lay hold of, and awaken the conscience; in which also the good Lord had respect to the desire of His

---

12. Ibid., 41.

servant; for I had not preached long, before some began to be touched, and be greatly afflicted in their minds at the apprehension of the greatness of their sin, and of their need of Jesus Christ.[13]

It was never lost on Bunyan that he was an unworthy and unprofitable slave of Christ who had merely done his duty (Luke 17:10). Whatever he possessed, he possessed by the grace of God alone. He knew he was an unlikely candidate for preaching effectively for Christ, but he also knew the grace of God could result in the most unlikely of saints being used for the glory of God in His Kingdom. Yes, he was untrained, unlearned, and unscholarly. What of it? It never stopped the crowds from rushing to him. Offor would comment on this:

> The God who gave the wish and the talent, soon opens a way to still more public usefulness. In most cases, they enter upon a course of study, to fit them for their momentous labours; but many of our most valuable ministers have, like Bunyan, relied entirely upon their prayerful investigation of the Scriptures. His college was a dungeon, his library the Bible; and he came forth with gigantic powers to grapple with the prince of darkness. No human learning could have so fitted him for this terrible and mysterious warfare.[14]

Bunyan's ability to preach was a gifting of the Lord. Thankfully, even when he desired to bury this talent, the Christians in Bedford refused to allow him to start digging that hole and encouraged him to preach the Word of God publicly. These encouragements God used to persuade the man to enter public ministry, just as he had been called to do. Praise the Lord that, though reluctant, he was eventually receptive to this outward calling from his brothers and sisters in Christ.

Let the reader note, however, that the Tinker's preaching was improving over the years as well. At first, he was prone to preach against the sins of men. He was heavy on the Law and the condemnation of man underneath the crushing wrath of God. But, after having experienced the great inner working of God's grace, and the calmness felt through assurance of

---

13. Ibid., 41.
14. Offor, *Grace Abounding to the Chief of Sinners, Works*, 41.

salvation, his preaching was altered, and he began to preach all of Christ to men. Finally, after coming to an understanding of the doctrine of union with Christ, his preaching matured further to focus on the great reality of the Christian's being joined together to Christ. He wrote the following of these three periods:

> In my preaching of the word, I took special notice of this one thing, namely, that the Lord did lead me to begin where His word begins with sinners; that is, to condemn all flesh, and to open and allege, that the curse of God by the law, doth belong to, and lay hold on all men as they come into the world, because of sin. Now this part of my work I fulfilled with great sense; for the terrors of the law, and guilt for my transgressions, lay heavy on my conscience: I preached what I felt, what I smartingly did feel; even that under which my poor soul did groan and tremble to astonishment...
>
> I went on for the space of two years, crying out against men's sins, and their fearful state because of them. After which, the Lord came in upon my own soul, with some staid peace and comfort through Christ; for He did give me many sweet discoveries of His blessed grace through Him; wherefore now I altered in my preaching (for still I preached what I saw and felt); now therefore I did much labour to hold forth Jesus Christ in all His offices, relations, and benefits unto the world; and did strive also to discover, to condemn, and remove those false supports and props on which the world doth both lean, and by them fall and perish...
>
> God led me into something of the mystery of the union of Christ; wherefore that I discovered and showed to them also. And, when I had travelled through these three chief points of the word of God, about the space of five years or more, I was caught in my present practice, and cast into prison...[15]

Bunyan's experience is likely similar to that of most preachers of the gospel. As the saint matures in Christ, so too do the sermons he preaches to his listeners. While the content may differ over time, or different subjects given a different

---

15. Bunyan, *Grace Abounding to the Chief of Sinners, Works*, 1:42.

emphasis, the passion for Christ and His Word only increases and grows all the stronger.

The Tinker Takes Up the Pen

Bunyan was more than just a gifted preacher, however. He was also, as we know by this point, a very gifted writer of everything from spiritual autobiographies, allegories, poetry, and theology. Even a simple reading of one of his sermons is profitable and, though none today has heard the Tinker's voice, his voice echoes throughout his sermons and other writings. One can almost close their eyes and hear his loud voice, in early modern English, ringing out with declarations of the truth of God's Word.

It may come as a surprise that Bunyan was already a published author by the time he was imprisoned, and long before he published *The Pilgrim's Progress*. In fact, his acceptance of his call into ministry coincides rather closely with his taking up the pen to begin writing. But what was it that made a relatively unlearned and unscholarly man desire to write? What moved him so?

As is so often the case with some of the best Christian writers, Bunyan took up the pen in order to defend biblical truths against those who would deny them. His first book, *Gospel Truths Opened*, was written as a direct response to those calling themselves *Quakers* who held to a number of distinct heretical teachings. Now, it must be noted that the Quakers, or Society of Friends, did not, as a group, hold to these heretical teachings. But Bunyan did come face to face with those calling themselves Quakers, and they most certainly held to the following heresies for themselves:

> 1. That the holy scriptures were not the word of God. 2. That every man in the world had the spirit of Christ, grace, faith, etc. 3. That Christ Jesus, as crucified, and dying 1600 years ago, did not satisfy divine justice for the sins of the people. 4. That Christ's flesh and blood were within the saints. 5. That the bodies of the good and bad that are buried in the churchyard, shall not arise again. 6. That the resurrection is past with good men already. 7. That that man Jesus, that was crucified between two thieves, on mount Calvary, in the land

of Canaan, by Jerusalem, was not ascended above the starry heavens. 8. That He should not, even the same Jesus that died by the hands of the Jews, come again at the last day; and as man, judge all nations, etc.[16]

Bunyan first dealt with these heresies publicly on Tuesday, May 23, 1656, in Bedford. He had likely just finished ministering to the Bedford Meeting when some itinerants came to town and, meeting with the Tinker in the parish church, discussed these doctrines of deep significance and importance. Offor notes that the subjects of 'holiness in this life' and 'whether it was lawful to perform the work of the ministry for hire,'[17] and, doubtless, other doctrinal disputes were discussed at this time as well.

Now, after having debated them in person, Bunyan lifted his pen because he saw the doctrine of God under attack, as well as the doctrine of Scripture, the doctrine of Christ, and the doctrine of salvation. These matters, for Bunyan, were so weighty and significant that he had little choice but to involve himself in a written and public exchange. Perchance, he thought, he could help others and grab them away from the fire of heresy, and then the writing of these gospel truths would be of all the greater value. Either way, as John Calvin once famously said, if a dog attacks when his master is attacked, what servants of Christ would we be if we saw Him attacked and remained quiet?

Bunyan was not of the temperament to pick fights, but he was of the mind to defend Christ and His Word against those who would assault it. In the chance that some may think Bunyan was simply trying to make a name for himself in attacking the doctrine of these so-called *Quakers*, let his own words speak for him when, in his letter to the reader of this work, he wrote:

> And indeed, who are the men that at this day are so deluded by the quakers, and other pernicious doctrines; but those who thought it enough to be talkers of the gospel, and grace of God, without seeking and giving all diligence to make it sure

---

16. Ibid., 1:21.

17. Offor, *The Editors Advertisement* to John Bunyan, *Some Gospel Truths Opened, Works*, 2:130.

unto themselves? 'And for this cause God' [shall send] hath sent 'them strong delusion, that they should believe a lie: That they all might be damned, who believed not the truth, but had pleasure in unrighteousness,' as it is written (2 Th. ii.11,12). And indeed if you mark it, you shall see, that they be such kind of people, who at this day are so carried away with the quakers' delusions; namely, a company of loose *ranters*, and light notionists, with here and there a legalist, which were shaking in their principles from time to time, sometimes on this religion, sometimes on that. And thus these *unstable souls* are deluded and beguiled at last (2 Pe. ii.14).[18]

His concern was not to make a name for himself, but to protect the glorious name of the Lord Jesus Christ against those who dubiously attacked those doctrines that are central to the Christian faith. But, even here, there is a sense of love and compassion shown on behalf of the Tinker toward his opponents, for he ends this work with a series of questions toward the Quakers, wherein he attempts to lead them into the truth of the Scriptures. The questions allow and even invite a response, but more importantly, these questions succinctly summarize both the main heresies he was fighting against, as well as the main points of Bunyan's text, once more pointing these deniers of doctrinal truths back to the truths of God's perfect and inerrant Word.

Now, it is also noteworthy that this first published work displays a genuine understanding of both the gospel and the Reformed doctrines of grace. Even at this relatively early stage in both his walk with Christ and Christian ministry, Bunyan held a firm grip on the sovereignty of God. Likewise, he also had a good understanding of the Covenant of Redemption, wherein, in eternity past, the Father, Son, and Spirit covenanted together to save a particular people from the entirety of the human race. It is helpful to see this early theological formation in Bunyan, and so here we will look at the opening paragraphs of *Some Gospel Truths Opened*, where he wrote:

> [God] knowing that man would break his commandments, and so throw himself under eternal destruction, did in his own purpose *fore-ordain* such a thing as the rise of him that should

---

18. Bunyan, *Some Gospel Truths Opened*, *Works*, 2:133.

fall, and that by a *Saviour*, 'According as he hath chosen us in him, (meaning the Saviour) before the foundation of the world.' Ep. i.4. That is, God seeing that we would transgress, and break his commandment, did before *choose* some of those that would fall, and give them to him that should afterward purchase them actually, though in the account of God, his blood was shed before the world was. Re. xiii.8. I say, in the account of God, his Son was slain! that is, according to God's purpose and conclusion, which he purposed in himself before the world was; as it is written (2 Tim 1:9), 'Who hath saved us, and called us with an holy calling, according to his own purpose and grace, which was given us in Christ Jesus before the world began.' As also, in 1 Peter 1:20, Where the Apostle speaking of Christ, and the redemption purchased by him for sinners, saith of him, 'Who verily was fore-ordained before the foundation of the world, but was manifest in these last days for you, who by him do believe in God, that raised him up from the dead.' God having thus purposed in himself, that he would save some of them that by transgression had destroyed themselves, did with the everlasting Son of his love, make an agreement, or bargain, that upon such and such terms, he would give him a company of such poor souls as had by transgression fallen from their own innocency and uprightness, into those wicked inventions that they themselves had sought out (Eccl 7:29). The agreement also how this should be, was made before the foundation of the world was laid (Titus 1:2). The Apostle, speaking of the promise, or covenant made between God and the Savior (for that is his meaning,) saith on this wise; 'In hope of eternal life, which God that cannot lie, promised before the world began.' Now this promise, or covenant was made with none but with the Son of God, the Saviour. And it must needs be so; for there was none with God before the world began, but he by whom he made the world, as in Proverbs 8 from verse 22 to verse 31 which was and is, the Son of his love.[19]

Bunyan's peculiar ability to explain the deep truths of the gospel in a succinct and winsome way is already clearly on display. Despite his lack of formal theological education, his years spent in deep contrition taught him to treasure the Scriptures. His deep meditation upon God's Word had taught

---

19. Ibid., 141-42. Some of the text has been lightly edited, as in the case of certain Scripture references Bunyan had made, for readability.

him how to handle, and teach, the Word of God in such a way that its unfathomable depths and infinite riches could be grasped by young and old, babes in Christ and the spiritually mature, alike.

The Great Wit of the Tinker

His wit is also on display at this early stage. In his follow up work, *A Vindication of Gospel Truths Opened*, some of his adversaries had responded to his first work. Evidently, they had been unable to formulate powerful arguments against the claims Bunyan had made based upon Scripture, so they had taken instead to attacking his character. They attempted to charge Bunyan of having preached only for money, stating that he, like the false prophets, had attempted to make merchandise of souls. Bunyan retorted:

> Friend, dost thou speak this as from thy own knowledge, or did any other tell thee so? However, that spirit that led out this way, is a lying spirit. For though I be poor, and of no repute in the world, as to outward things; yet through grace I have learned by the example of the apostle to preach the truth; and also to work with my hands, both for mine own living, and for those that are with me, when I have opportunity. And I trust that the Lord Jesus, who hath helped me to reject the wages of unrighteousness hitherto, will also help me still, so that I shall distribute that which God hath given me freely, and not for filthy lucre's sake. Other things I might speak in vindication of my practice in this thing: but ask of others, and they will tell thee that the things I say are truth: and hereafter have a care of receiving anything by hearsay only, lest you be found a publisher of those lies which are brought to you by others, and so render yourself the less credible; but be it so.[20]

Bunyan was a poor Tinker, and any examination of his life at this point in time would have revealed how laughable such claims of greed for filthy lucre actually were. But, rather than just laugh at the false claims, the Tinker made it a point to answer the charge with wit, and then lovingly correct his accuser.

---

20. John Bunyan, *A Vindication of Gospel Truths Opened*, *Works*, 2:201.

Bunyan's writings, when engaging in debate, were often like this. Take, as another example, his short 1673 treatise *Differences in Judgment About Water Baptism, No Bar to Communion*. Here, the problem lay with his fellow Baptists and the question was whether or not those who had not been baptized after conversion were permitted to hold membership or partake of the Lord's Supper. William Kiffen, with whom the Tinker had possibly met in London during one of his preaching excursions, was the chief agent of the assault against him. Bunyan's practice was to allow an 'open' communion table in that all who made an open profession of Jesus Christ as Lord and Savior were allowed to participate, regardless of whether they were baptized after conversion. The only ones barred from the table were those who had not made a profession of faith. Others, like Kiffen, unsatisfied with Bunyan's approach, challenged him in his practice.

First, in the opening letter to his readers, Bunyan explains:

> Be intreated to believe me, I had not set pen to paper about this controversy, had we been let alone at quiet in our Christian communion. But being assaulted for more than sixteen years, wherein the brethren of the baptized way, as they had their opportunity, have sought to break us in pieces, merely because we are not, in their way, all baptized first... That I deny the ordinance of baptism, or that I have placed one piece of an argument against it, though they feign it, is quite without colour of truth. All I say is, That the church of Christ hath not warrant to keep out of their communion the Christian that is discovered to be a visible saint by the word, the Christian that walketh according to his light with God. I will not make reflections upon those unhandsome brands that my brethren have laid upon me for this, as that I am a machivilian, a man devilish, proud, insolent, presumptuous, and the like, neither will I say as they, The Lord rebuke thee; Words fitter to be spoken to the devil than a brother.[21]

Bunyan had been assaulted by his fellow Baptists, he wrote, for sixteen years, before finally taking up the pen in this debate. They had misinformed others of his own practices and

---

21. Bunyan, *Differences About Water Baptism, No Bar to Communion*, *Works*, 2:616-17.

beliefs, hurled terrible insults at him (some even suggesting that he had many mistresses and was secretly a Jesuit),[22] and had even called for the Lord to personally rebuke him. All this, the Tinker took in his stride. Even here, his aim was not so much to defend himself or his character, but to defend what he believed to be doctrinal truths.

Probably a great deal of Baptists reading this will disagree with Bunyan's approach, just as those Baptists of his own day did.[23] But it does seem that twelve years spent in prison had taught the Tinker some wisdom in handling such matters and, right or wrong, he believed himself to be right. His enemies and debaters could say what they would of the Tinker, but they could never accuse him of not being true to his conscience as bound to Scripture.[24]

Yet, despite the Tinker's amiable attitude toward those of differing opinions and debating attitudes, he was not afraid to write with a pen dripping with wit. In his response to a preface written by William Kiffen within Thomas Paul's *Some Serious Reflections on that Part of Mr. Bunion's Confession of Faith: Touching Church Communion with Unbaptized Persons* of 1672, Bunyan opens with the following paragraph:

> Your seemingly serious reflections upon that part of my plain-hearted confession of faith, which rendereth a reason of my freedom to communicate with those of the saints and faithful who differ from me about water baptism; I have read and considered, and have weighed them so well as my rank and abilities will admit me to do. But finding yours, if I mistake not, far short of a candid replication, I thought [it] convenient, not

---

22. Offor noted that, "When he was defamed, his slanderers called him a witch, or fortune teller, a Jesuit, a highwayman, or the like." Offor, *Grace Abounding to the Chief of Sinners, Works*, 1:2.

23. I, for one, disagree with Bunyan. While I appreciate his sincere convictions, I believe he was sincerely wrong in this matter, and I would side with the Particular Baptists. While I do not believe Bunyan can be counted among "Particular Baptists" in this sense, he most certainly did hold to baptistic and Calvinistic teachings. One must genuinely engage his arguments from Scripture, but it does him no disservice to note his inaccuracies in this area, either.

24. It does no disservice to Bunyan to disagree with him. As many have noted, even the best of men are still men at best. Personally, I believe the Particular Baptists held the more biblically compelling argument, but even in disagreement, we can still learn from the Tinker.

only to tell you of those impertinencies everywhere scattered up and down in your book; but also, that in my simple opinion, your rigid and church-disquieting principles are not fit for any age and state of the church.[25]

Bunyan knew he was outranked, whether academically, socially, or economically, by his opponents, and he was not about to deny their specialty in the field of theology. But he also knew that, as simple as he and his confession were, that he was filled with the Holy Spirit and could ably interpret the Bible. Therefore, he would engage in such a debate, sharing his opinion, and showing where he found Kiffen's book to be most lacking.

And, yet, Christ's love is on great display as Bunyan writes, 'What Mr. Kiffin hath done in the matter I forgive, and love him never the worse, but must stand by my principles because they are peaceable, godly, profitable, and such as tend to the edification of my brother, and as I believe will be justified in the day of judgment.'[26] There really may be no better insight into Bunyan's mind and heart than this one simple line: Even as he was ridiculed and attacked by those he counted as allies, he was quick to forgive and continue to love.

Pastoring, Preaching, and Writing During Trials

Bunyan's life was like a rollercoaster of highs and lows. Just when he finally found assurance of salvation, he met with the heretical doctrines of those calling themselves *Quakers*. After the birth of his daughter Mary, who was blind, in 1650, his second child, Elizabeth, was not born until 1654. The next year, in 1655, John moved his family to St Cuthberts St, Bedford, and John Gifford passed away soon thereafter on 21 September, 1655. Records of the baptisms of Bunyan's children, while infants, seem to indicate that his first wife had remained loyal

---

25. Bunyan, Differences About Water Baptism, No Bar to Communion, Works, 2:617.

26. Ibid.

to the Church of England, even as he sought fellowship within Gifford's Bedford Free Church.[27]

With the passing of his friend and mentor, John Gifford, he found a new mentor in John Burton, who took over the pastorate after the passing of Gifford, in 1656. That same year, his first son, Thomas, was born, and his first book, *Some Gospel Truths Opened*, was published. The next year saw the birth of his second son, John, and his start as deacon. In 1658, his first wife passed away, leaving John with four children to attend to, raise, and care for, by himself.

While many of his enemies often used his lack of education against him, and others tried to intimate that he only preached and wrote for fame and money, the truth was that the Tinker had multiple reasons to quit and give up. Perhaps most men in his shoes would have. Yet, even after being threatened, ordered to stop preaching, and eventually jailed, John remained steadfast in his calling before the Lord.

He was a man of conviction and passion. While he refused to trifle in the affairs of those things that would take his eyes from Christ, or purposefully disrupt the unity of the brethren, he would always rise in defense of Christ, trumpeting from pen and pulpit the old truths. From his own pen, he explained, 'I never cared to meddle with things that were controverted, and in dispute amongst the saints, especially things of the lowest nature; yet it pleased me much to contend with great earnestness for the word of faith and the remission of sins by the death and suffering of Jesus.'[28]

What was the Tinker's secret? Where did his strength to continue preaching and writing come from in the midst of such torrential storms and heavy rains in his life? The answer, of course, is that he, like the Apostle Paul, had learned the secret of true contentment. 'I know both how to be abased, and I know how to abound: every where and in all things I am instructed both to be full and to be hungry, both to

---

27. When one considers his stance on open membership and communion, perhaps it should be unsurprising that he permitted his children to be baptized as infants. Though Bunyan was a Baptist, it may not be wrong to refer to him as an inconsistent Baptist.

28. Bunyan, *Grace Abounding to the Chief of Sinners*, *Works*, 1:43.

abound and to suffer need. I can do all things through Christ which strengtheneth me' (Phil. 4:12-13). Bunyan could preach and write during heavy persecution and vast trial because he knew Christ personally, and it was Christ who gave him strength and contentment to keep fighting the good fight of faith.

CHAPTER 5

Persecution of the Puritan: Bunyan as a Nonconformist during the Great Ejection

Then Apollyon broke out into a grievous rage, saying, 'I am an enemy to this Prince; I hate His person, His laws, and people. I am come out on purpose to withstand thee.'

Christian: 'Apollyon, beware what you do, for I am in the King's highway, the way of holiness: therefore take heed to yourself.'

Then Apollyon straddled quite over the whole breadth of the way, and said, 'I am void of fear in this matter. Prepare thyself to die; for I swear by my infernal den, that thou shalt go no farther: here will I spill thy soul.'

And, with that, he threw a flaming dart at his breast; but Christian held a shield in his hand, with which he caught, and so prevented the danger of that.

(Christian does battle with Apollyon, *The Pilgrim's Progress*)

'Yea, and all that will live godly in Christ Jesus shall suffer persecution' (2 Tim. 3:12). It is true, for every follower of Jesus, that there is a cost to following Christ (Luke 9:57-62,

115

14:28). Taking up the cross to follow Jesus means that, at the very least, persecution will follow. After all, if they hated the Master, how could the slaves expect to receive better treatment than Him? As Jesus explained in John 15:18-27, since the world hated Him first, we can expect the world to hate us.

Persecution, however, may take different forms at different times. For the early Christians, persecution often resulted in martyrdom, and it still does for most of the world today. On the other hand, in the West, persecution for the past few centuries has, for the most part, consisted of little more than verbal abuse and missing out on job promotions. While persecution may be increasing, and the forms of attack are becoming more severe, it is important to note that every generation deals with these attacks, to one degree or another. Bunyan's generation was no different. The Puritans, as a whole, and nonconformists, in particular, were a major target for both church and state, as they were united in the established Church of England.

Abuses from Those Around Him

Bunyan, like the long line of godly saints before him, was no stranger to persecution and he experienced varying degrees of it for almost the full duration of his Christian pilgrimage on earth. We have already noted, in the previous chapter, how some of Bunyan's enemies took to insulting his intelligence, his lack of formal education, and even accused him of being like Simon the Sorcerer, seeking only to make money and fame through the name of Christ. He explained that slander was regularly employed against him in order to do harm to his ministry, and 'It began therefore to be rumoured up and down among the people, that I was a witch, a jesuit, a highwayman, and the like.'[1]

These insults, having failed to accomplish the ruin of the Tinker's public reputation, were left off and new slanderous insults adopted. 'That which was reported with the boldest confidence, was, that I had my misses, my whores, my bastards; yea, two wives at once, and the like.'[2] These slanderous lies were just that: Lies. They were lies constructed to become

---

1. John Bunyan, *Grace Abounding to the Chief of Sinners*, *Works*, 1:45.
2. Ibid.

rumors that would ruin Bunyan's ministry. But, on every account, they fell woefully short of the truth, and he was vindicated on all such accounts.

We are able to trace at least one of these rumors to their source. It appears that, on one occasion, Bunyan happened upon a Mrs. Agnes Beaumont. She desired to attend a meeting but was running late. Bunyan, approaching on horseback, spotted the young lass and her brother. Her brother asked if the Tinker could carry her on horseback and, she recorded, 'Mr. Bunyan answered, with some degree of roughness, "No, I will not carry her."'[3] But they pressed on him, insisting that, if he did not give her a ride on horseback, she would become most miserable and broken-hearted. Eventually, he agreed to allow her to ride behind him. This decision was enough to cause quite the stir. First the girl's father, upon finding out, was greatly flustered and ran after Bunyan, intending to pull his daughter from the horse. Later, Mr. Lane in Bedford spotted the two riding and began to spread the rumor that the two were in a scandalous relationship with one another. Of course, there was no truth to the scandal, but such rumors as these seem to have been a common source of vexation for the Tinker.

Besides those insults that he regularly was forced to endure from within the ranks of Christians, there were the daily struggles of his home life to contend with. His daughter, Mary, was blind and his wife passed away in 1658, leaving him to care for four children on his own. As he worked as a tinker to support his family, he also worked as a father at home, fulfilling the role of nurturer and caregiver—a striking opposite to his own father and lack of care he had received as a child.

At the same time, he fought against heretical teachings with his books and treatises, aiming to make certain that the teachings of the church at large remained pure and orthodox, especially in their doctrines of God and salvation. This was, in itself, a great matter that required the Tinker's focus and time. But, there were other battles to be fought still.

---

3. George Offor records this account, taken from James' *Abstract of the Gracious Dealings of God with Several Eminent Christians.* See: *Grace Abounding to the Chief of Sinners, Works,* 1:45.

For many of the Puritans, they feared the Church of England had very quickly become as bad, if not worse, than the corrupted Roman Catholic Church that their Reformation forefathers had fought against only a century prior. While many Puritans had fled to the new world to escape religious persecution from the church and Crown, those who stayed were locked in a bitter fight to secure the right to worship as God commanded in His Word, rather than how some governing authority commanded worship to be done.

The English Civil War was, in large part, a war between Protestants. The Puritans, and especially the Congregationalists/Independents of Cromwell's New Model Army, refused to commit themselves to the rule and structure of the Church of England.

The Act of Uniformity

After the execution of Charles I in 1649, Oliver Cromwell became Lord Protector in 1653, until his death in 1658. During this time, Puritanism enjoyed its lengthiest period of peace and prosperity. Cromwell had refused the title of king, declaring that if God had seen fit to destroy the crown and lay it in the dust, he would not take it back up again. Thus, religious freedom was enjoyed for about the span of a decade, despite the English Civil War continuing for a few years until 1651. (Roman Catholics were excluded from the religious freedom and toleration, but other groups, like Presbyterians, Congregationalists, Baptists, Levelers, and even the Fifth Monarchy Men all thrived during these years.)

The war effort had, however, left a mark. One sect of Christians, the Fifth Monarchy Men, believed the return of Jesus Christ was imminent and sought to establish a government of godly saints in preparation of the Lord's return. They had believed, according to a bad interpretation of Daniel 2, that the execution of Charles I had brought the fourth monarchy to an end and all that was left was to establish a final monarchy for Cromwell to become king. They had fought alongside Cromwell to see the reign of Charles I brought to an end, but turned against him when he refused himself to become king and established the Protectorate instead.

With problems existing amongst the Protestants as a whole and even the Puritan groups, the tumultuous period was about to become even more dangerous for the likes of Bunyan when Cromwell passed away in 1658. Only a few months later, in May of 1659 and under the leadership of Cromwell's son Richard, the Protectorate collapsed. Richard was unable to secure the support of the army and internal divisions ensued. It seemed that he simply was not the leader that his father was. General George Monck, commanding the English forces in Scotland, marched back to London to restore order. But order was all but gone and the Protectorate had failed. The golden age of Puritanism was coming to an end. On 8 May, 1659, Parliament declared King Charles II the rightful heir to the crown. Furthermore, they determined that he had been unlawfully excluded from the kingdom; Parliament believed he was the lawful king since the death of his father in 1649.

The public crowning of Charles II did not take place for another two years. But on 23 April, 1661, the monarchy was completely restored as he was publicly crowned at Westminster Abbey. The great diversity that had existed amongst the Puritans was now going to be one of the direct causes of an explosion of persecution.

At first glance, the waters that would soon turn tumultuous still seemed calm, and storm clouds seemed a long way off. Bunyan's ministry as a preacher was being firmly established and he found himself preaching more and more. In fact, between his work as a tinker, his writing, his preaching engagements, and his family, he soon had to step down from being a deacon within the Bedford Meeting. Offor notes:

> The employment of his time in earning a maintenance for his family, and his constant engagements to preach, interfered with the proper fulfillment of his duties as a deacon of the church. His resignation of this important office is thus recorded in the minutes of the church — 'At a meeting held on the 27th of the 6th month, 1657, the deacon's office was transferred from John Bunyan to John Pernie, because he could no longer discharge its duties aright, in consequence of his being so much employed in preaching.'[4]

---

4. Offor, *Memoir of John Bunyan, Works,* 1:xxxvii.

In 1659, a year after the death of his first wife, Bunyan married Elizabeth. He was a thirty-one-year-old widower, with four children, and she was only eighteen. Yet, something had brought the two together and it seemed they were destined for happy times. His children would now, once again, have a mother to care for them, and the Tinker would have a wife and helpmeet. But their happy marriage was soon turned upside down.

Still, there was some evidence of what would soon come. Bunyan had begun to travel to different locations to preach and knew the trouble that would come with doing so. As he explained, 'When I went first to preach the Word abroad, the doctors and priests of the country did open wide against me.'[5] Those who were licensed by the Church of England were apparently the most prone to attacking him. Yet, it was during these years that he likely first came into contact with the reputable Puritan John Owen, who would be instrumental in having Bunyan released from prison during his second stay.

The first true signs of trouble arose in 1658 when, for the first time, Bunyan was indicted for preaching without a license from the Church of England, though he avoided imprisonment at this time. This occurred in Eaton Socon, not far from Bedford, when he was thirty years old. The following year, he was accosted by a Mr. Thomas Smith, a Cambridge scholar, who began to publicly attack and ridicule the Tinker's ministry. It seems that, like those who indicted Bunyan, he likewise was troubled that John had no license to preach. His aggressive attacks also included the typical assaults against Bunyan's lack of education and trade as a tinker.

On this occasion, a fellow Baptist, Henry Denne, who had been a licensed preacher within the Church of England before joining himself to the General Baptists, came to Bunyan's defense. He wrote to Mr. Smith:

> But I found it [Smith's letter against Bunyan] so confused, that I have desisted to prosecute that resolution; you seem to be angry with the Tinker because he strives to mend Souls as well as Kettles and Pans: and you are so angry, that your passion clouded your reason, and made you forget what you had to do:

---

5. Bunyan, *Grace Abounding to the Chief of Sinners, Works*, 1:42-43.

the main drift of your Letter is to prove that none may preach except they be sent (and you do that also lamely). Sir I think him unworthy the name of a Tinker that affirms that any one is sufficient to preach the Gospel without sending. By your confession the Tinker thinks otherwise, and doth not deny what you labour to prove; and so you contend with a shadow: he pleads his Mission and Commission from the Church at Bedford; it behoves you to prove either that this is false, and that the Church at Bedford never gave such a Commission, or else that the Church is not in a capacity to give such a Commission. You should also have proved that Mr. Thomas Smith hath a better Commission from some other Church, then [sic] the Tinker either hath or can have from the Church at Bedford. This would have drawn the acceptation of your friends. And it is a task worthy your labour, to send forth your determinations concerning the questions which are thus stated, by many of your friends.[6]

Indeed, if the worst of charges his enemies could bring against him was that he was a mender of both the souls of men and kettles and pans, then the Tinker was an exemplary Christian. But these attacks were evidence of the trials that were yet to come.

One of Bunyan's largest problems was the Act of Uniformity of 1558 (not passed by Parliament until 1559), an Act intended to regulate the liturgy of the Church of England. In accordance with this Act, the Anglican *Book of Common Prayer* was to be used in the church's liturgy to establish union amongst sister churches. Likewise, all had to attend a service of the Church of England at least once a week or face a fine of about three days' worth of wages. Other Acts were then made over the next century or so, and each would be detrimental for the Puritans, and especially Bunyan.

However, this Act was basically repealed on 27 September, 1650, by the newly established commonwealth of England, under Lord Protector Cromwell's reign. This meant that the early years of Bunyan's ministry saw no conflict with the law.

---

6. Henry Denne, *THE QUAKER NO PAPIST, in Answer to The Quaker Disarm'd. OR, A brief Reply and Censure of Mr. Thomas Smith's frivolous Relation of a Dispute held betwixt himself and certain Quakers at Cambridge* (London, 1659). https://ota.bodleian.ox.ac.uk/repository/xmlui/bitstream/handle/20.500.12024/A81304/A81304.html?sequence=5&isAllowed=y

However, when the monarchy was reinstituted under King Charles II, the previous repeal was counted as null and void. The Acts that before had no effect on Bunyan now began to rear their heads.

With the repeal counted as null and void, the Act of Uniformity of 1558 and multiple other Acts now impacted Bunyan and the Bedford congregation. One of these Acts that so affected Bunyan, as we have already seen in his indictment and Thomas Smith's challenge to him, was actually passed on 26 April, 1645. It read: 'None may preach but ordained ministers, except such as, intending the ministry, shall, for trial of their gifts, be allowed by such as be appointed by both houses of Parliament.'[7]

Following Charles I's deposal, an amendment to the Act was made under Cromwell's commonwealth. 'This was amended by "an ordinance appointment commissioners for approbations of public preachers," March, 1653.'[8] Evidently, other Puritans like Dr. John Owen, Thomas Goodwin, and Joseph Caryl 'were to judge of the candidates fitness to preach.'[9] (Amusingly enough, these 'Triers,' as they were called, as high-Calvinists, were given the nicknames, 'Dr. Absolute, chairman, Mr. Fatality, Mr. Fri-babe, Mr. Dam-mam, Mr. Narrow-grace, Mr. Indefectible, Mr. Dubious, and others.')[10]

If these had been the only Acts and Amendments in view, considering Owen's favorable and amicable disposition toward the Tinker, Bunyan may have still been able to thrive under them. However, the Act of 2 May, 1648, which was reinstituted under Charles II, the persecution against Bunyan all the more severe because, though apparently enacted by Puritans, it specifically targeted Baptists. This Act enacted a law against those who would insist on the practice of credobaptism (believer's baptism). It stated that any person who taught, 'that man is bound to believe no more than by his reason he can comprehend, or that the baptising of infants is unlawful, or such baptism is void, and that such persons ought to be

---

7. Offor, *Memoir of John Bunyan*, *Works*, 1:XLI.

8. Ibid.

9. Ibid.

10. See: Footnotes, 2, of *Memoir of John Bunyan*, *Works*, 1:XLI.

baptised again, and, in pursuance thereof, shall baptise any person formerly baptised, shall be imprisoned until he gives security that he will not publish or maintain the said error any more.'[11] These were the Acts that would see the persecution of such venerable Baptists as William Kiffen, Edward Barbour, and Vavasor Powell.

The worst of the persecution erupted in 1662. This was the year that the *Book of Common Prayer* was updated, and the second Act of Uniformity was passed. This was really an extension of what had been attempted with the 1558 Act of Uniformity. The 1662 Act was stronger in some of its language, but much of the same was expected: Public prayers had to follow the *Book of Common Prayer* (which, being reworked the same year, meant that most Christians were completely unfamiliar with the contents thereof and what was being imposed upon them), and all other rites and sacraments were to be performed as outlined within. Furthermore, all ministers, whether deacons, priests, or bishops, had to receive episcopal ordination from the Church of England.

Thousands of others suffered under the re-establishment of the monarchy, and specifically under the new Act of Uniformity of 1662. That same year, the Great Ejection occurred. The Act was designed knowing that the Puritans would not consent to the ordinances being forced upon them. Their expulsion was all but guaranteed.

It is impossible to cover all the details of the Great Ejection in a work focusing primarily on Bunyan. Iain H. Murray is correct in his assessment that, 'Any serious consideration of the cause and consequences of the Ejection must carry us far beyond the confines of a single year.'[12] It is worth recognizing, however, that on St Bartholomew's Day (August 24) in 1662, two thousand ministers of the gospel were ejected from their positions within the Church of England for refusing to conform with the new demands being placed upon them. Many dissenters would later refer to this as 'Black Bartholomew's Day,' noting that the date coincided with the Bartholomew's

---

11. Ibid.

12. Iain H. Murray, *Sermons of the Great Ejection*, (Edinburgh, UK: The Banner of Truth Trust, 1962), vii.

Day Massacre of 1572.[13] Of those ejected, notable Puritans include Richard Baxter, Thomas Manton, Thomas Watson, John Flavel, and Thomas Brooks.

Arrested for Preaching

Bunyan was not serving within the Church of England, but he was an obvious target even before the Act of Conformity of 1662 was passed. His arrest would occur in 1660, two years before the Great Ejection would occur. The establishment of the monarchy meant that any number of previous Acts could be used against the Tinker. He had received some notoriety with the writing of his books and tracts, and many had traveled to hear the Tinker preach. The Bedford Free Church (or Meeting), during Cromwell's commonwealth era, had shared the facilities of St John's Church in Bedford alongside an Anglican congregation. Now, that would no longer be possible. Forced out, Bunyan and the congregation had to meet in more private settings.

On 12 November, 1660, Bunyan was warned that there was a warrant for his arrest. He had already been meeting with the Bedford congregation secretly, on farms, in barns, and wherever they were able to without fear of duress. Having been invited on this particular day to preach at Lower Samsell in Bedfordshire, he had all intentions to go and preach, until the warning came to him.

What would he do? He was newly married, and Elizabeth and their four children, one blind, depended on him. He desired to be a present and loving father. Could he be faulted from fleeing from the place? If the authorities could not find him, he could continue to live with his family. After all, he had already been indicted once, but allowed to continue preaching. He had, so far, escaped their persecution. Was it not right for him, now that he knew what to expect, to flee from the persecution to come?

The decision was not made lightly, but Bunyan chose to suffer affliction with the people of God, bearing the reproach of Christ (Heb. 11:25-26), rather than run from the tribulation.

---

13. Bartholomew's Day Massacre was a massacre carried out by Roman Catholics upon French Huguenots.

His plan was to preach on John 9:35, wherein Jesus asks the man whom He has healed of blindness, who has been cast out of the synagogue, 'Dost thou believe on the Son of God?'

Sir Francis Wingate, of Harlington House, was the Justice who issued the warrant for Bunyan's arrest. Because of his 'secret' meetings, Bunyan was considered as having broken the Conventicle Act of 1593, which explicitly forbade religious gatherings of more than five people (outside of family) outside of the parish church.

Some of the justices thought field preaching so unlawful, they equated it with regicide, which is the act of killing a king. According to Offor, 'One of the informers [of field preachers], named W. S., was very diligent in this business; "he would watch a-nights, climb trees, and range the woods a-days, if possible to find out the meeters, for then they were forced to meet in the fields."'[14] Whoever had been the informant in this case was, evidently, no friend to the Puritans.

Even after his friends had warned him against attending the meeting at Lower Samsell in Bedfordshire, Bunyan was resolute. He recorded that, when his friend asked whether it was necessary to meet that day, his response to cancel the meeting had been, 'No, by no means, I will not stir, neither will I have the meeting dismissed for this. Come, be of good cheer; let us not be daunted; our cause is good, we need not be ashamed of it; to preach God's Word, is so good a work, that we shall be well rewarded, if we suffer for that; or to this purpose.'[15]

When the constable made his way to the meeting, he found Bunyan and the others gathered without weapons, with no plans of treason in view. Rather, they simply held their Bibles in hand, prepared to worship the Lord and hear His Word proclaimed. Bunyan recalled:

> Alas! the constable, when he came in, found us only with our Bibles in our hands, ready to speak and hear the word of God; for we were just about to begin our exercise. Nay, we had begun in prayer for the blessing of God upon our opportunity, intending to have preached the word of the Lord unto them

---

14. Offor, *Memoir of John Bunyan*, *Works*, 1:xlvii.

15. Bunyan, *Relation of Bunyan's Imprisonment*, *Works*, 1:51.

there present: but the constable coming in prevented us. So I was taken and forced to depart the room.[16]

The Tinker's View of Authority

When most hear the word 'dissenter' today, they think of one who is regularly opposed to authority. It is even likely that most think of those who are generally rebellious and seek opportunities to withstand those in authority over them.

Bunyan was far from a typically rebellious figure. In fact, though he was a nonconformist/Dissenter, his problem was not with those figures in authority placed over him, but with their ungodly commandments which restrained the proper worship of God. In fact, Offor noted that:

> When he was apprehended for neglecting to attend the church service and for preaching the gospel, in his conversation with Mr. Cobb, the magistrate's clerk, he said 'that, to cut off all occasions of suspicion from any, as touching the harmlessness of my doctrine, in private I would willingly take the pains to give any one the notes of all my sermons, for I do sincerely desire to live quietly in my country, and to submit to the present authority.'[17]

Even when the constable came to arrest him, he did not attempt to flee or fight back against him. He simply allowed himself to be led away, entrusting himself into the sovereign care of God Almighty. Likewise, when speaking with the Clerk of the Peace about the insurrectionists in London during the Venner Rebellion (a Fifth Monarchist revolt led by Thomas Venner in January of 1661), the Tinker responded, 'That practice of theirs, I abhor, said I; yet it doth not follow that, because they did so, therefore all others will do so. I look upon it as my duty to behave myself under the King's government, both as becomes a man and a Christian, and if an occasion were offered me, I should willingly manifest my loyalty to my Prince, both by word and deed.'[18]

---

16. Ibid.
17. Offor, *Memoir of John Bunyan, Works*, 1:xxxvii.
18. Bunyan, *Relation of Bunyan's Imprisonment, Works*, 1:57.

Now, it is true that some of Bunyan's writings connect him to that radical millenarian group known as the 'Fifth Monarchists,' but even with this connection, it is hard to view the Tinker as a generally rebellious figure. Richard L. Greaves noted this connection within Bunyan's *The Advocateship of Jesus Christ*. Greaves explained:

> Near the end of this work Bunyan recalled that 'I did use to be much taken with one Sect of Christians, for that it was usually their way, when they made mention of the Name of *Jesus*, to call him, *The blessed King of Glory*.' Upon reflection— in a climate charged with tenson as hostility to James II mounted—Bunyan calmly observed that 'Christians should do thus; 'twould do them good.' He was not, of course, suggesting a revival of the Fifth Monarchy movement, but reminding his readers that their ultimate sovereign was Christ, not James II.[19]

Bunyan did not suggest the deposition of Charles II, even though he had, at least in a small sense, fought with Parliament once before to see the removal of his father, Charles I. In fact, his disposition seems to have been to generally submit to the rule of his government as placed above him by God. But, when the governing authorities attempted to introduce laws that would effectively make the proper worship of God impossible, Bunyan's response was that 'We ought to obey God rather than men' (Acts 5:29).

His demonstration in this matter is very much that of the motto, 'Obey God, defy tyrants.' Bunyan believed that his ordination to preach the gospel, as having been called by the Bedford Church, was just as valid as those licensed by the Church of England. He believed that he ought to have been allowed the freedom to pray extemporaneously, rather than be bound to the written prayers of the *Book of Common Prayer*. While he had no aspirations to overthrow the Crown, he did desire for Christians to remember that their true King is Christ alone, and therefore obedience to Him is to be kept above all else.

---

19. Richard L. Greaves. 'John Bunyan and the Fifth Monarchists.' *Albion: A Quarterly Journal Concerned with British Studies* 13, no. 2 (1981): 83-95. https://doi.org/10.2307/4049043.

Bunyan, and the majority of the Nonconformists, were not violent revolutionaries, seeking to take up the sword and enact violent and bloody vengeance upon their enemies. They harbored no secret motive to use bloodshed to bring about a new Christendom. Instead, they were patient reformers. They truly believed that obeying Christ, preaching the Word, worshiping Jesus, praying to their sovereign God, and gathering together for Christian fellowship would, ultimately, change the world. They knew the promise of Jesus that 'the meek shall inherit the earth' (Matt. 5:5), and thus understood patience was a virtue in this spiritual battle. One day, their King would return to the earth, having had all enemies placed beneath His feet (Ps. 110:1), the nations having been discipled (Matt. 28:19), and He would strike down His remaining enemies with sword in mouth (Rev. 19:15). Vindication and vengeance would ultimately belong to Him alone (Ps. 26:1, 43:1, 94:1). Bunyan and the Nonconformists knew their enemies were not of the flesh and blood variety but consisted mainly of spiritual principalities in high places (Eph. 6:12). Thus, they would endure their hardships patiently through prayer and faithfulness to God, trusting that the good Lord in His sovereignty would deal justly with them and bless the generations still to come.

Vavasor Powell, around this same time, also being persecuted for being a Baptist, wrote an extraordinary hymn entitled, 'To Christ our King.' It seems that the words of this hymn are a testimony to the beliefs of many of the Puritan Nonconformists and, likely, contains language that Bunyan himself would have fancied:

> TO Christ our King, let us praise sing,
> who is our Saviour dear,
> Who is our Protector, and our Rock,
> who will come, and soon appear
> To humble his, and try their hearts,
> And make them clean and pure,
> To set his Kingdom upon Earth,
> Which ever shall endure:
> His Saints shall reign with him on Earth,
> And great ones then shall bow,

The Battle, and the Battle-ax,
And men of War shall know
That he will arise, and he will rule,
And their power will fall,
And Christ our great Commander, He
Shall be our General.
Hast Lord, come quickly down,
Thy Saints, do wait, and pray,
And men would faign, if they knew how,
Thy Prophets kill and slay:
But they shall live, and eke stand up,
And give their Testimony
Against the Monarchs of the Earth,
That sit, and reign on high.[20]

Bunyan's Trial

Bunyan knew that he had to stand his ground. This was no time for cowardice. It is always better to obey God rather than man (Acts 5:29) and the saint standing upon the promises of Christ will be enabled to stand firm against even the most tumultuous of waves. But, if he fled or buckled under the pressure of an impending trial, what would people say of him? What would his enemies say of the church? What would sinners say of Christ? Bunyan thought of all this and more as he was arrested:

> I thought, that seeing God of His mercy should choose me to go upon the forlorn hope in this country; that is, to be the first, that should be opposed, for the gospel; if I should fly, it might be a discouragement to the whole body that might follow after. And further, I thought the world thereby would take occasion at my cowardliness, to have blasphemed the gospel, and to have

---

20. Vavasor Powell, 'To Christ our King.' Found within Alexander Griffith, *Strena Vavasoriensis,: a Nevv-Years-gift for the Welch itinerants, or a hue and cry after Mr. Vavasor Powell, metropolitan of the itinerants, and one of the executioners of the Gospel, by colour of the late Act for the propagation thereof in Wales; as also a true relation of his birth, course of life, and doctrines; together with a vindication of several places of Scripture wrested and abused, against the present government, and all publick ministers of this nation. His hymn sung in Christ-Church London; with an antiphona there unto; and a lively description of his propagation* (London: F.L., 1654), 24. https://quod.lib.umich.edu/e/eebo2/A856 96.0001.001/1:4?rgn=div1;view=fulltext

had some ground to suspect worse of me and my profession, than I deserved.[21]

As he was led away from the meeting, he encouraged those who had gathered with him to stand firm and to be of good cheer, for they were being persecuted for the cause of Christ, and there was no greater reason to suffer. Their weight of glory in eternity would be all the richer.

That day, Bunyan was placed under the charge of a friend, for Justice Wingate was not at home. But, the very next morning, Bunyan was brought before Wingate to be tried. First, Wingate questioned whether the meeting had been found to be in possession of any weapons, but finding this not to be the case, he was taken further aback to find that those who had met together had truly only met together to hear the Word of God preached.

Wingate, at this point, is said to have asked the Tinker, 'What I did there? And why I did not content myself with following my calling? for it was against the law, that such as I should be admitted to do as I did.'[22] Bunyan's answer is both resolute and courageous. It is an encouragement to every Christian, and especially those who have been called to preach the gospel. 'The intent of my coming thither, and to other places, was to instruct, and counsel people to forsake their sins, and close in with Christ, lest they did miserably perish; and that I could do both these without confusion (to wit), follow my calling, and preach the Word also.'[23] What a testimony! Oh, that the Lord would raise up more preachers of this caliber who, in the face of being threatened, would resolutely declare their allegiance to Christ and desire to see souls saved from their sin!

Wingate was flustered. He threatened to break the neck of Bunyan's meetings, and Bunyan admitted, 'It may be so.'[24] Did Bunyan believe that his church would be ended? Perhaps he did; what he did not believe, however, was that Wingate or Satan himself would ever bring the Church of Jesus Christ to

---

21. Bunyan, *Relation of Bunyan's Imprisonment, Works*, 1:51.
22. Ibid.
23. Ibid.
24. Ibid.

an end. He knew that, ultimately, this battle was against the gates of hell, which could never hope to prevail against Christ or His Church but would one day be trampled to the ground (Matt. 16:17-19). What an amazing display of bravery in the face of persecution and prolonged imprisonment!

At this point, Wingate was prepared to release Bunyan still, if only the Tinker would swear to stop preaching. Lesser men may have accepted the bargain, promising to never again preach. But not Bunyan. He would not stop preaching; on the contrary, he swore to continue to preach. When Peter and John stood trial before the religious authorities and were ordered to quit preaching, they answered, 'Whether it be right in the sight of God to hearken unto you more than unto God, judge ye. For we cannot but speak the things which we have seen and heard' (Acts 4:19-20). Bunyan's response to such bargaining was cut from the same cloth:

> When the bond for my appearance was made, he told them, that they was bound to keep me from preaching; and that if I did preach, their bonds would be forfeited. To which I answered, that then I should break them; for I should not leave speaking the Word of God: even to counsel, comfort, exhort, and teach the people among whom I came; and I thought this to be a work that had no hurt in it: but was rather worthy of commendation, than blame.[25]

Wingate withdrew for a time and in entered a Dr. Lindale, who took to taunting the Tinker. Here we have quite the scene: An apparently learned doctor, snidely taunting the lowly Tinker for his lack of learning and inability to secure a license from the Church of England. But Bunyan would not take the bait and refused the argument. He merely quoted the Scriptures in response. His opportunity to serve Christ well under great persecution would not be made ruin of because of a few tempting words from the enemy.

Lindale's questioning related to Bunyan's license to preach. The Tinker answered that, as it is written in 1 Peter 4:10, the one who has received the gift is to minister the same. This, Bunyan argued, applied to all who had been given the gift

---

25. Ibid., 1:51-52.

to preach, and not merely those who had received licensure through the Church of England. In fact, licensure from the Church of England meant very little to the Tinker in light of his calling from God to preach and minister the gospel.

Lindale then attempted to compare the Tinker to Alexander the Coppersmith, who, in a similar vocation to Bunyan, had opposed the Apostles and their teaching. But rather than answer him further, John remembered it best not to answer the fool according to his folly (Prov. 26:4). Dr. Lindale could hurl all manner of cruel and vicious insults against the Tinker, and the Tinker would gladly accept them all, for 'Blessed are ye, when men shall revile you, and persecute you, and shall say all manner of evil against you falsely, for my sake. Rejoice, and be exceeding glad: for great is your reward in heaven: for so persecuted they the prophets which were before you' (Matt. 5:11-12). Sharing in the suffering and reproach of Christ was a burden that Bunyan was glad to carry.

Eventually, Wingate returned with the constable to deliver Bunyan to prison, but as they made their way to the jail, they were stopped by two of the Tinker's friends. They convinced the constable to wait, believing they could secure Bunyan's release. After some time, they returned with the good news that, if he would now go and speak again to Wingate, he would not be sent to prison.

On the way back to the Justice, Bunyan met with a Mr. Foster from Bedford. This exchange was strange to the Tinker, for Foster expressed a great deal of love and affection for Bunyan, though they were hardly even acquaintances. Even stranger still, Foster was a known persecutor of the Puritans and their cause. Bunyan's suspicions were well founded.

As it turned out, Foster was not truly a friend of Bunyan, but one more tempter who sought to bring an end to his ministry. After Bunyan had explained that he was arrested for assembling together with intent to preach the Word of God, the exchange is recorded as follows:

> Fost. So (said he), I understand: but well, if you will promise to call the people no more together, you shall have your liberty to go home; for my brother is very loath to send you to prison, if you will be but ruled.

Bun. Sir (said I), pray what do you mean by calling the people together? my business is not anything among them, when they are come together, but to exhort them to look after the salvation of their souls, that they may be saved, etc.

Fost. Saith he, We must not enter into explication, or dispute now; but if you will say you will call the people no more together, you may have your liberty; if not, you must be sent away to prison.

Bun. Sir, said I, I shall not force or compel any man to hear me; but yet, if I come into any place where there is a people met together, I should, according to the best of my skill and wisdom, exhort and counsel them to seek out after the Lord Jesus Christ, for the salvation of their souls.[26]

This exchange soon followed the familiar pattern of insulting John's learning and academic experience, as Foster began to accuse Bunyan of bad hermeneutics, mishandling of the texts of Scripture, and ignorance of God's Word because he knew not how to read Greek. When no serious sin has been committed, it is often the case that the enemies of Christ will gripe at the lowest hanging fruit available. But such assaults were common by this point to the Tinker and could hardly faze him anymore.

Foster eventually left after hurling the same tired insults that many others had, and several servants of Wingate came to Bunyan. They praised the Justice's kindness and, once more, tempted Bunyan to quit preaching by explaining that the Tinker could go free if only he would no longer call together meetings. The Tinker explained that he really had not called together the meetings, but merely preached when Christians met together; furthermore, what was meant by calling people together? What if, in the public square, people were called to assemble to hear the reading of some book or other? Could he not then speak to a group gathered in any area? Could he not read the Scriptures aloud to friends? Could he not preach if the Lord Himself said, 'Preach!'?

Recognizing that the Tinker would not take the offer, both Foster and Wingate returned to have him sent to prison.

---

26. Ibid., 52-53.

Foster was actually the one who insisted that Bunyan be sent to prison, and like a cowardly Pilate, Wingate consented to send him away. But, despite the terrible sentence before him, the Tinker went away with the peace and calmness of God in his heart. He would carry out his sentence by the grace of God.

None would be blamed for being of low spirits at this point. But Bunyan expressed a different attitude altogether:

> I was not at all daunted but rather glad, and saw evidently that the Lord had heard me; for before I went down to the justice, I begged of God that if I might do more good by being at liberty than in prison, that then I might be set at liberty; but if not, His will be done; for I was not altogether without hopes but that my imprisonment might be an awakening to the saints in the country, therefore I could not tell well which to choose; only I, in that manner, did commit the thing to God. And verily, at my return, I did meet my God sweetly in the prison again, comforting of me and satisfying of me that it was His will and mind that I should be there.[27]

The good news for Bunyan, though he would now be imprisoned, is that religious prisoners were allowed particular privileges. For example, his family was allowed to visit and bring him one meal a day. On other occasions, he was actually allowed out of his jail cell and his jailers permitted him to go and minister to his congregation. Most importantly, he was allowed his writing supplies.

Productive Imprisonment(s)

George Whitefield once remarked of Bunyan's life:

> Ministers never write or preach so well as when under the cross; the Spirit of Christ and of glory then rests upon them. It was this, no doubt, that made the Puritans ... such burning and shining lights. When cast out by the black Bartholomew-act [the 1662 Act of Uniformity] and driven from their respective charges to preach in barns and fields, in the highways and hedges, they in an especial manner wrote and preached as

---

27. Ibid., 1:54.

men having authority. Though dead, by their writings they yet speak; a peculiar unction attends them to this very hour.[28]

Strange as it may be, Bunyan was terrifically fruitful for the Lord and His Kingdom during his prison stay. He worked as a tinker, repairing shoelaces to provide money for his family at home. At the same time, he wrote and published various tracts and books that gained some renown. Of this first prison stay, his most influential work was his autobiography, *Grace Abounding to the Chief of Sinners*.

It was also during this time he had the chance to stand before several Justices for the quarter-session to be tried. The charges leveled against him here were as follows:

> That John Bunyan, of the town of Bedford, labourer, being a person of such and such conditions, he hath (since such a time) devilishly and perniciously abstained from coming to church to hear Divine service, and is a common upholder of several unlawful meetings and conventicles, to the great disturbance and distraction of the good subjects of this kingdom, contrary to the laws of our sovereign lord the King, etc.[29]

Bunyan made it clear, in no uncertain terms, that he saw no reason to attend the parish church because he was a member of God's Church, and regularly met together with Christians. When the Justices challenged him that he was commanded by God's Word to pray, and therefore should have attended the parish services, Bunyan admitted that praying was commanded, but not with the prayers of *The Common Prayer Book*. He was a firm believer in extemporaneous prayer, as led by the Spirit of God within (1 Cor. 14:15). *The Common Prayer Book*, in Bunyan's view, was to be opposed because God's Word commanded prayer by the Spirit with understanding, and not by the Spirit and *The Common Prayer Book*. These were the prayers of men; prayers which, when they prayed, were fine for them. But if he felt compelled to pray from the heart and in the moment, then Bunyan believed it to be his right to

---

28. George Whitefield, *Works* (London, 1771), IV:306f. Found within J.I. Packer, *A Quest for Godliness: The Puritan Vision of the Christian Life* (Wheaton, Il: Crossway, 1990), 23.

29. Bunyan, *Relation of Bunyan's Imprisonment, Works*, 1:54.

do so. As he insisted, Romans 8:26 promised the Holy Spirit would lead to prayer with understanding at the proper times, even when the saints knew not what to pray, and that God had promised without the need of *The Common Prayer Book*.

Amusingly, it became clear that, though the Tinker was the unscholarly and unlearned one, the Justices were overwhelmingly outmatched by his wisdom and knowledge of Scripture. When the examination came to an end, Bunyan declared that, should he be released, he would immediately go and preach the gospel again the next day.

When Bunyan later met with Mr. Cobb, the Clerk of the Peace, on 3 April, 1661, he was again told to simply stop meeting and he could go free. Again he refused. Once more, the challenge was then leveled against his ability to preach. How could Cobb, or any other, determine if he was really able to preach?

Bunyan challenged Cobb, or any other, to listen to his preaching and determine whether or not God had gifted him in such a way. Cobb asked, 'But will you be willing that two indifferent persons shall determine the case; and will you stand by their judgment?' To which Bunyan asked, 'Are they infallible?' When Cobb responded that they were not, Bunyan answered, 'Then it is possible my judgment may be as good as theirs. But yet I will pass by either, and in this matter be judged by the Scriptures; I am sure that is infallible, and cannot err.'[30]

It was this commitment to the Word of God, ultimately, that would lead him to stay in prison. He refused to sin against God or His Word. During this time, he would continue to work on his writing.

The Bunyan Family during John's Imprisonment

By August of 1661, Bunyan had petitioned the judges to be heard at least three times through his wife. A short note, then, is necessary regarding his wife during this time of imprisonment.

Back at home, Elizabeth was left to care for the four children of Bunyan's previous marriage. This she appears to have done with the nurturing love and gusto of a true

---

30. Ibid, 59.

mother. At the same time, she began to work tirelessly to try and secure her husband's release from prison. It is remarkable that, having been married for a short time and only around twenty or twenty-one years of age, Elizabeth was resolute in her attempts to petition the judges.

She traveled the nearly sixty-mile journey from Bedford to London to petition the Earl of Bedford to release her husband. This same month, she went before Judges Hale and Twysden, within the Swan Chamber. A Justice Chester was also present, and nearly scared her away when he spoke of her husband as a rambunctious troublemaker. But, steadying her beating heart, she stood before the Judges and the Justice and made her plea.

While her attempt to free her husband failed, one part of her conversation with these men will here be recorded in order to show her tenacity in working for the release of her husband:

> My Lord, said she, I was a while since at London, to see if I could get my husband's liberty; and there I spoke with my lord Barkwood, one of the House of Lords, to whom I delivered a petition, who took it of me and presented it to some of the rest of the House of Lords, for my husband's releasement; who, when they had seen it, they said, that they could not release him, but had committed his releasement to the judges, at the next assizes. This he told me; and now I am come to you to see if any thing may be done in this business, and you give neither releasement nor relief.[31]

Though release seemed impossible, the same temptation reared its head once more. Judge Twysden offered his release if only he would stop preaching. Elizabeth bravely responded, 'My Lord, he dares not leave preaching, as long as he can speak.'[32] Though they were unable to secure his release, his family stood tirelessly by his side to encourage him in his ministry, even while imprisoned.

It was during his arrest and imprisonment that Elizabeth miscarried her first child with John. The stress proved to be great upon the young woman. But, being allowed to visit her husband in jail, and he being allowed leave by kind jailers on occasion, Elizabeth gave birth to their daughter, Sarah,

31. Ibid., 61.
32. Ibid.

in 1666. Following this was the birth of their son, Joseph, in 1672. This would be the year Bunyan finally was released from prison, under the 'Quaker Pardon,' which he was able to take advantage of.

While imprisoned, he was also regularly visited by his eldest daughter, Mary. The familial heart of Bunyan is on display in his writings here, as he makes known his close relationship and deep love for both his eldest daughter and other children. He wrote:

> I found myself a man and compassed with infirmities; the parting with my wife and poor children, hath often been to me in this place, as the pulling the flesh from the bones, and that not only because I am somewhat too fond of these great mercies, but also because I should have often brought to my mind the many hardships, miseries, and wants that my poor family was like to meet with, should I be taken from them, especially my poor blind child, who lay nearer my heart than all besides: Oh! the thoughts of the hardship I thought my poor blind one might go under, would break my heart to pieces.[33]

The whole family sacrificed during the entire duration of his imprisonment, and, indeed, during the entirety of his ministry. This they did, not only out of love for one another, but out of love for the Lord Jesus Christ.

Unfortunately, this first imprisonment was not the last. Though it lasted twelve years, another was to come. Bunyan was imprisoned a second time, in 1676 to 1677, for a total of six months. This time, it was because he again had refused to attend what the government had ordained as the official 'parish church.' It was during this second stint that the Tinker dreamed a dream that would effectively become the basis of his most famous and perhaps most important work, *The Pilgrim's Progress*. Even with this second stay, the Tinker proved to be fruitful in his work.

Bunyan's friend, the Puritan John Owen, was one of the main reasons this second prison stay was cut short. The friendship between the two was surprising for a number of reasons, not least of which being that they were two completely different men, with Owen held in high regard by society and Bunyan

---

33. Bunyan, *Grace Abounding to the Chief of Sinners*, *Works*, 1:48.

esteemed the lowest of the low, but they were united by their brotherhood in Christ. In fact, while Owen was able to avoid the more negative effects of the Acts of Uniformity due to his high position in society, he never shied away from attempting to help those who were suffering for the sake of Christ, and especially exerted his influence to try and aid Bunyan. As his biographer, Andrew Thomson, wrote:

> There was no sufferer in whose behalf Owen exerted his influence more earnestly than John Bunyan. It is well known that, as a preacher, Bunyan excited, wherever he went, an interest not surpassed even by the ministry of Baxter. When he preached in barns or on commons, he gathered eager thousands around him; and when he came to London, twelve hundred people would be found gathered together at seven on the dark morning of a winter working-day, to hear him expound the Word of God. Among these admiring multitudes Owen had often been discovered; — the most learned of the Puritans hung for hours, that seemed like moments, upon the lips of this untutored genius... For some years Bunyan's confinement in the prison of Bedford had, through the kindness of his good jailer, been attended with many mitigations; but towards the latter part of it, its severities had been greatly increased, and Owen used every effort to engage the interest of his old friend and tutor, Dr Barlow, for his release... It is pleasing to know, that after some perplexing delay, Owen's interposition was successful in obtaining Bunyan's enlargement.[34]

Owen may not have suffered in the same ways Bunyan did, but he was willing to participate in the sufferings of the Tinker he respected so much by pleading for his release. It was with the second prison stay that Owen's influence proved most valuable in obtaining the Tinker's release. As Edmund Venables explained, 'This last imprisonment of Bunyan's lasted only half as many months as his former imprisonment had lasted years. At the end of six months he was again a free man. His release was due to the good officers of Owen, Cromwell's celebrated chaplain, with Barlow, Bishop of Lincoln.'[35]

---

34. Andrew Thomson, *Life of John Owen*, in *Works of John Owen* (Edinburgh, UK: Banner of Truth Trust, 1965), 1:XCII.

35. Edmund Venables, *The Life of John Bunyan*, Project Gutenberg Edition, 2005, transcribed from 1888 Walter Scott Edition.

Still, even in his imprisonment, Bunyan worked. And that work, especially within *The Pilgrim's Progress*, has stood the test of the centuries. This demonstrates to Christians what happens when 1 Corinthians 15:58 is followed: 'Therefore, my beloved brethren, be ye stedfast, unmoveable, always abounding in the work of the Lord, forasmuch as ye know that your labour is not in vain in the Lord.' Laboring for the Lord, whether under heavy persecution or not, is never in vain. The work we do for the Kingdom of God, whatever our lot in life, counts for eternity. Therefore, Bunyan's resolute steadfastness teaches us to stand steadfast in Christ always.

CHAPTER 6

The Pastoral Heart of the Shepherd: Bunyan's Tender Care for the Flock In and Out of Prison[1]

Now, when they were got almost quite out of this wilderness, Faithful chanced to cast his eye back, and espied one coming after him, and he knew him. 'Oh!' said Faithful to his brother, 'who comes yonder?' Then Christian looked, and said, 'It is my good friend Evangelist.' 'Ay, and my good friend, too,' said Faithful; 'for it was he that set me the way to the gate.' Now was Evangelist come up unto them, and thus saluted them:

Evangelist: Peace be with you, dearly beloved, and peace be to your helpers.

Christian: Welcome, welcome, my good Evangelist: the sight of thy face brings to my thought thy former kindness and unwearied laboring for my eternal good.

Faithful: 'And a thousand times welcome,' said good Faithful: 'thy company, O sweet Evangelist, how desirable is it to us poor pilgrims!'

---

1. Some of the material in the following chapter first appeared on *Meet the Puritans*, part of *Reformation 21*, but has been edited and adapted by the author for usage within the context of this chapter.

Evangelist: Then said Evangelist, 'How hath it fared with you, my friends, since the time of our last parting? What have you met with, and how have you behaved yourselves?'

Then Christian and Faithful told him of all things that had happened to them in the way; and how, and with what difficulty, they had arrived to that place.

Evangelist: 'Right glad am I,' said Evangelist, 'not that you met with trials, but that you have been victors, and for that you have, notwithstanding many weaknesses, continued in the way to this very day. I say, right glad am I of this thing, and that for my own sake and yours. I have sowed, and you have reaped; and the day is coming when "both he that sowed and they that reaped shall rejoice together;" that is, if you faint not. The crown is before you, and it is an uncorruptible one: so run that you may obtain it. Some there be that set out for this crown, and after they have gone far for it, another comes in and takes it from them: "Hold fast, therefore, that you have; let no man take your crown."'

(Christian and Faithful meet once more with Evangelist, *The Pilgrim's Progress*)

It has often been the case that the most ignoble of characters and chief of sinners become the best of Christians. Seemingly, the greater the past life of sins, the deeper the misery before Christ, the more that soul will labor all the more abundantly and diligently for the Kingdom of God, and this most certainly was the case in the life of John Bunyan. His conversion was one of extremes. As we already noted, even more shocking than his former life of sin for many was that he was a relatively unlearned and unscholarly man. This was often used as fuel for the fire of his persecution. Friends, comrades, and enemies alike could not help themselves, at certain times, from grabbing hold of the low-hanging fruit of his education. But his life, perhaps more than any other, proves that old adage true, 'God does not call the equipped, but He does equip the called.'

Nothing about those early years of the Tinker would have led one to believe that Bunyan would later in life develop the heart of a pastor, let alone become one of the most influential Christians in the English-speaking world. Fewer still would have imagined that he would spend a good portion of his life under heavy persecution and in prison.

In this chapter, we will reflect on how Bunyan tenderly cared for the flock that the Lord entrusted to his care. At the same time, because the two events overlap and coincide a great deal, we will also examine his imprisonment and learn how the Tinker handled these trials. As we will see, even while he was imprisoned, the Lord was working in various ways that Bunyan would later recognize as providential.

Calling People Out from Sin to Christ as One Called Out from Sin by Christ

John 6:44 found full expression in the life of Bunyan: 'No one can come to me unless the Father who sent me draws him' (ESV). From his own admission, he wanted nothing to do with Christ. Having been taught how to curse and swear by his father, he became proficient at the use of vulgarities. He engaged in wonton sinfulness and deviancy.

But, Bunyan had learned the deep power of the conviction of the Holy Spirit. As Jesus promised, 'And when he comes, he will convict the world concerning sin and righteousness and judgment' (John 16:8 ESV). After conversion, he had become a man of a great many convictions. At the forefront of these convictions was the all-important and powerful desire to not deny Christ or His Word. This had led him to prison and would be his driving force while he continued there.

The Lord would continue His sovereign work on Bunyan while he was in prison, calling him to a greater denial of himself and his own wants and a greater faith in Christ. God had already used Bunyan's first wife, Gifford's preaching of the Word, and other events like these to draw the lost sinner to Himself. Though, by his own admission, he had tried to earn his own righteousness for some time, and boasted in himself when others applauded his new morality, it would eventually be thoughts of the new birth that would lead to his own conversion. Having recognized his own deplorable and wretched condition, and after honestly assessing himself and seeing no evidence of the new birth having taken place, he finally repented and trusted in Jesus as his Lord and Savior. Now, in prison, he was allowed a great deal of time for self-examination and the jail cell he occupied would operate as his own university classroom, with the Bible and *Foxe's Book of Martyrs* his professors and textbooks.

Like the Apostle Paul before him, Bunyan had learned to rejoice in Christ and despise his sin in equal measure. Just as the Apostle, growing closer to Christ and wiser with age, saw his own depravity all the more, so too did Bunyan. As Paul wrote first of being the least of the Apostles (1 Cor. 15:9), then the least of the saints (Eph. 3:8), and finally the chief of sinners (1 Tim. 1:15), Bunyan saw himself as a great sinner who had experienced abounding grace from the Lord. And, truly, what born-again Christian has not experienced this very thing? The most effective pastors, it would seem, are those who love the Lord and despise their sin, recognizing naught of good have they done, but all their righteousness is found in Jesus alone.

Though *The Pilgrim's Progress* would not be written until his second prison stay, this work is a marvelous example of not only Bunyan's own conversion (though allegorical, the work has much overlap with his own autobiography), but it also serves as an example of the heart of the sinner, who once was lost but had been found by Christ, now imploring others to come to Christ as well.

While in prison, his writing output continued to increase. *Profitable Meditations* was written in 1661, with *Prison Meditations* and *Christian Behaviour* following in 1663. He expanded upon doctrines like election, the resurrection of the dead, and the order of salvation. He also penned *Grace Abounding* while in prison, in 1666, and wrote his own defense and confession of his faith. Other works followed, but probably the most valuable from this time is *Grace Abounding*, which served as a spiritual autobiography in the same vein as Augustine's *Confessions*.

Tinker, Soldier... Preacher?

When one pauses to think about the nature of Bunyan's life, amazement is the result. The man went from a ringleader of sinners, to soldier in the English Civil War, to Tinker, and, finally, to famed Christian writer and pastor. While he was in prison, his fame continued to grow. He was allowed, by some jailers, the opportunity to leave his jail cell. (This is every bit as strange and unusual as it sounds, and can only be chalked up to the grace of God over the Tinker's life.) On these occasions, he would go and meet with the saints and preach the Word of God. As amazing as it may seem, George Offor related, within the *Memoir*, that Bunyan's midnight preaching birthed many of the Baptist churches in and around Bedford. It is impossible, from our earthly perspective, to determine what impact Bunyan's preaching had on the planting of Baptist churches around the world.

The changes in Bunyan from his days as a lost sinner to a born-again Christian are profound. However, keep in mind, his background did not lend itself well to preaching. After all, the preacher is one who must dutifully study the Scriptures, but Bunyan had to have his first wife help him read the Christian works she had bought him. A preacher must be warm and gentle toward the sheep, but violent toward the wolves; hardly the behavior one could expect from a wretched youth turned solider turned infamous town sinner.

Yet, as the Lord would have it, Bunyan had a penchant for preaching that made him quite effective in ministry. This was undeniable even while he was imprisoned. In fact, there is an anecdotal account that even his friend, the great John Owen, once remarked that he would willingly trade all of his knowledge if he could simply preach like that tinker, John Bunyan.

What was it that made Bunyan so effective at communicating? Three things: His sincerity, sobriety, and simpleness. He was sincere when he presented the gospel, sober in his communication, and simple in his expositions of God's Word.

Though there are a number of works that could be examined in order to understand his style of communication, one of his more well-known statements comes from a book he penned entirely on John 6:37, entitled *Come and Welcome to Jesus Christ: A Plain and Profitable Discourse on John 6:37. Showing the cause, truth, and manner of the coming of a sinner to Jesus Christ; with his happy reception and blessed entertainment.* Like most Puritan titles from the time, it really rolls off the tongue. It also clues the reader in so that they are very much aware of what the contents of the work will be. Thus, it is no surprise to come across such an urgent, passionate, and warm invitation for sinners to receive Christ. He writes:

> From the largeness and openness of the promise: 'I will in no wise cast out.' For had there not been a proneness in us to 'fear casting out,' Christ needed not to have, as it were, waylaid our fear, as he doth by this great and strange expression, 'In no wise;' 'And him that cometh to me I will in no wise cast out.' There needed not, as I may say, such a promise to be invented by the wisdom of heaven, and worded at such a rate, as it were on purpose to dash in pieces at one blow all the objections of coming sinners, if they were not prone to admit of such objections, to the discouraging of their own souls. For this word, 'in no wise,' cutteth the throat of all objections; and it was dropped by the Lord Jesus for that very end; and to help the faith that is mixed with unbelief. And it is, as it were, the sum of all promises; neither can any objection be made upon the unworthiness that thou findest in thee, that this promise will not assoil.

> But I am a great sinner, sayest thou. 'I will in no wise cast out,' says Christ. But I am an old sinner, sayest thou. 'I will in no wise cast out,' says Christ. But I am a hard-hearted sinner, sayest thou. 'I will in no wise cast out,' says Christ. But I am a backsliding sinner, sayest thou. 'I will in no wise cast out,' says Christ. But I have served Satan all my days, sayest thou. 'I will in no wise cast out,' says Christ. But I have sinned against light, sayest thou. 'I will in no wise cast out,' says Christ. But I have sinned against mercy, sayest thou. 'I will in no wise cast out,' says Christ. But I have no good thing to bring with me, sayest thou. 'I will in no wise cast out,' says Christ.

Thus I might go on to the end of things, and show you, that still this promise was provided to answer all objections, and doth answer them.[2]

Clearly, John 6:37 was an important text to Bunyan, and was a verse he treasured deeply. It reads, 'All that the Father gives me will come to me, and whoever comes to me I will never cast out' (ESV). No doubt Bunyan had not only experienced the great joy of being received into the embrace of Christ, despite his numerous past sins, he had also experienced the delightful assurance of knowing that nothing would ever cause Christ to cast him away, nor would anything separate him from the love that he had discovered in Christ his Lord.

This exposition of John 6:37—an urgent, yet warm, call for sinners to repent of their sin and come to Christ—is standard to all of Bunyan's sermons and writings. Like the prophet Isaiah, he was one who had been commissioned to preach the gospel after having been confronted with the depravity of his own wickedness and the astonishing holiness of God. In turn, he understood deeply the great grace he had been gifted in Christ, and he was not one to squander it. Rather, he would use every moment and every ounce of strength to preach this same gospel to others.

Learning to Love the Communion of the Saints

While one may find many pastors who love the Lord, it is an unusual blessedness to find a pastor who loves his congregation as well. Many simply join a church with the intention of eventually moving on to greener and greater pastures. But, for Bunyan, the congregation of Bedford was one he cared for deeply. As the writer of Ecclesiastes wrote, there truly is nothing new under the sun; it was just as difficult in Bunyan's day to find true worshipers of God who loved the Lord and the people of God alike. But the Tinker was one of these priceless specimens of godly love.

The Tinker was a man who loved both the Lord and His Church. He had learned this great love, first, from the

---

2. John Bunyan, *Come and Welcome to Jesus Christ: A Plain and Profitable Discourse on John 6:37*, *Works*, 1:279-80.

women he had met that fateful day in Bedford and later increased in this love as he grew more acquainted with the Bedford congregation.

On that one fateful day, Bunyan recognized within those Bedford women something he had been missing: Joy. He also recognized where the source of the joy he found within these women originated: with Christ. These ladies had been drawn to Christ in salvation and had come to find the reality of their own wretched, miserable condition, and, at the same time, the perfect blessedness of Christ. It was from this river of joy that their words rushed forth. It was from this river of joy that Bunyan's own preaching would spring forth, as well.

As we saw, the impact on Bunyan was striking. As he would soon discover, these women were members of the Bedford Free Church, which he had joined before imprisonment. A few years before persecution would come against both himself and the church, he had served for some time as their deacon. But it was this first encounter with these women that would cause him to fall in love, not only with theology, but with the Lord and His people.

It has been often stated that doxology will never rise higher than theology. The two are always connected. But, let it also be said that a pastor's success in pastoring the flock entrusted to his care will never rise higher than the love, devotion, and care that he shows to that flock. As an undershepherd in Christ's flock, Bunyan's success as a writer, evangelist, preacher, and pastor can all be traced back to his observance of these two commandments: 'And you shall love the Lord your God with all your heart and with all your soul and with all your mind and with all your strength.' The second is this: 'You shall love your neighbor as yourself.' There is no other commandment greater than these' (Mark 12:30-31 ESV). The man who does not love the Lord simply cannot love the people of God, but the man who does not love the people of God proves He does not love the Lord (1 John 4:20).

Loving God's Church became a reality in Bunyan's life when he learned the true joy of knowing Christ and being known by Him. First broken over his sin, he found in Christ a mercy and grace that was rich and sweet. Seeing this same joy in others caused him to grow in love all the more for the congregation of Bedford.

Absent in Presence, Fond in Heart

It is no secret that John Bunyan was imprisoned for his faithful preaching of the Word of God during a time when faithfully preaching the Word of God *could* get one imprisoned. As a Nonconformist, Bunyan had joined the Bedford Meeting in the 1650s. Though he became a regular preacher, both publicly and at their secret meetings, he would not actually become their pastor until 1672—while he was still imprisoned. It is interesting to note that those within Bedford seemed to know something of which the Tinker was not himself privy to: that the laws enacted through the Acts were going to become laxer. They voted him their pastor on 21 January, 1672, a full four months before his release in May of that year.

Despite his imprisonment and powerful non-conformist preaching, one must not make the mistake of thinking that Bunyan was merely a preacher who lacked the heart of a pastor. On the contrary, he cared greatly for the congregation of Bedford and, though imprisoned, continued to fondly recall them in thoughts and prayers. (Let it be noted again that during the years of his imprisonment, he was given multiple opportunities to leave his jail cell, visit his family, and visit the congregation. Though not yet their pastor, he certainly ministered to them as often as he could.)

Like the Apostle Paul before him in Colossians 2:5,[3] Bunyan saw himself standing in spiritual solidarity with the Bedford congregation. This is perhaps most clear in the preface to his autobiography, *Grace Abounding to the Chief of Sinners*. He opens the work with these words to his congregation:

> CHILDREN, grace be with you, Amen. I being taken from you in presence, and so tied up, that I cannot perform that duty that from God doth lie upon me to youward, for your further edifying and building up in faith and holiness, etc., yet that you may see my soul hath fatherly care and desire after your spiritual and everlasting welfare; I now once again, as before,

3. 'For though I am absent in body, yet I am with you in spirit, rejoicing to see your good order and the firmness of your faith in Christ.' (ESV)

from the top of Shenir and Hermon, so now from the lions' dens, from the mountains of the leopards (S. of Sol. 4.8), do look yet after you all, greatly longing to see your safe arrival into the desired haven.[4]

Truthfully, one may also read these words as though he had passed away and had prepared this preface as a letter to his congregation, and perhaps that was his intention. However, one gets the immediate sense that Bunyan was of the caliber of noble pastors who, though facing harsh persecution and distress, cannot help but think of the needs of his congregation. Perhaps it was this deep longing and care for his flock that endeared him so greatly to his people that, while in prison, they voted him their pastor.

Reflection on Imprisonment

While in prison, friendships were made and hard lessons were learned.

In 1670, Nehemiah Coxe found himself in prison with Bunyan. Coxe was the famed Particular Reformed Baptist who helped to create what would later become known as the Second London Baptist Confession of Faith in 1677 (commonly referred to simply as the 1689, signifying the date the Confession was affirmed by a number of Particular Baptist congregations). The two likely remained in prison together for at least a year.

Not much is known of what conversations they may have engaged in during this time, but Bunyan's work *A Confession of My Faith* reveals at least one point of disagreement that we have already seen: Bunyan allowed those who had not been baptized as believers to partake of the Lord's Supper when most Baptists, like Coxe, would never dream of such a thing. This evidences the peculiar nature of Bunyan who was willing to oppose whosoever he imagined to stand in the opposition of God's Word. In fact, though he was a Baptist, and though he possessed friends who were both Particular Baptists and General Baptists, he likely would not have fully identified himself with either group. He was far too Reformed for the

---

4. Bunyan, *Grace Abounding to the Chief of Sinners*, *Works*, 1:4.

General Baptists to accept him, and yet too ecumenical and too broad in his ecclecisology for the Particulars.

Prison, if anything, seems to have taught Bunyan a great deal of wisdom to stand for what truly mattered, which often means standing alone. The important thing was that he stood for Christ. Many of his writings evidence that he was not looking to be popular, but true to God and His Word. Sometimes this meant he was wrong in his conclusions or practices. But his aim was to be biblical, and this must be the aim of every believer in Christ, even as we recognize not one of us is perfect. There is always more repenting and reforming to be done.

Bunyan, while in prison, recognized that his time there would be used as an instrument and rod of learning for both himself and others. Therefore, he would need to learn to suffer rightly. He wrote:

> By this scripture I was made to see that if ever I would suffer rightly, I must first pass a sentence of death upon every thing that can be properly called a thing of this life, even to reckon myself, my wife, my children, my health, my enjoyment, and all, as dead to me, and myself as dead to them. The second was, to live upon God who is invisible, as Paul said in another place; the way not to faint, is to 'look not at the things which are seen, but at the things which are not seen; for the things which are seen are temporal, but the things which are not seen are eternal.'[5]

An example of this is witnessed during his stay in prison. One day, it fell to Bunyan to preach to the inmates of the Bedford prison, but words seemed to fail him. He was disquieted, and a deep melancholy had overwhelmed him. So, what was the Tinker to do? Go to the Word, of course! 'However, looking through his Bible, he came upon the description of the heavenly Jerusalem at the end of the book of Revelation. His soul was dazzled by the splendor of God among His heavenly people. He took up the text with prayer, and he preached it

---

5. Ibid., 48.

with such power that he later enlarged it into a book, *The Holy City: or the New Jerusalem* (1665).[6]

He had learned an important truth: God's Word is the source of all wisdom and strength for even the most downcast and wearied.

Not Many Wise, Not Many Noble, Not Many Powerful

Bunyan's life was one used mightily by the Lord and both his family and flock were greatly blessed by his earnest strivings for the Kingdom of God. Indeed, centuries later, Christians continue to benefit greatly from his writings, especially *Pilgrim's Progress*. But what is most striking about Bunyan's life is that both pastor and laity can learn a simple lesson, first taught in Scripture. As the Apostle Paul in 1 Corinthians 1:26-31 writes, 'For consider your calling, brothers: not many of you were wise according to worldly standards, not many were powerful, not many were of noble birth. But God chose what is foolish in the world to shame the wise; God chose what is weak in the world to shame the strong; God chose what is low and despised in the world, even things that are not, to bring to nothing things that are, so that no human being might boast in the presence of God. And because of him you are in Christ Jesus, who became to us wisdom from God, righteousness and sanctification and redemption, so that, as it is written, "Let the one who boasts, boast in the Lord"' (ESV).

Bunyan was, before conversion, perhaps a least likely candidate for pastoral ministry. He was foolish and sinful, even by worldly standards, shameful, despised, and lowly; but God took this man from the miry clay and set his feet upon the solid rock of Jesus Christ. Bunyan's life was proof that the one who boasts must boast only in the Lord.

Pastors: Learn from the humility of Bunyan to lead your flock well. He was a simple preacher who reached many with the simple truths of God's Word. Preach to the congregation that is present, and not with the aim that others would think mightily of you. He was a simple man who earnestly desired to share the rich truths of Scripture that he loved so deeply with

---

6. Joel R. Beeke and Paul M. Smalley, *John Bunyan and the Grace of Fearing God* (Philipsburg: P&R Publishing, 2016), 21.

his hearers. If he seemed a fool for so doing, then he would all the more gladly bear that reproach if it meant calling sinners to Christ. He loved the fellowship of the saints and longed to not only see that number grow, but to see the number present grow in sweet communion. Yet, every success was answered with boasting in Jesus Christ alone. He kept one thought central: Grace had abounded to him, the chief of sinners. Let us, like Bunyan, continually cling to these same truths.

What makes John Bunyan so attractive is his love for the Lord and his love for fellow brothers and sisters. Make certain that your affections are set on Christ. Love the people of your local church, knowing that the Lord is producing within you all an eternal weight of glory. Therefore, run the race well.

And, should you find that you have a pastor like Bunyan, then here is what you must do: Pray for him, praise the Lord for him, and boast in Jesus Christ, who is the true Shepherd and overseer of all His elect.

CHAPTER 7

Preacher Par Excellence: The Extraordinary and Exceptional Expositional Preaching of the Tinker

Christian: And what said Faithful to you then?

Hopeful: He bid me go to Him and see. Then I said it was too much for me to ask for. But he said No, for I was invited to come. Then he gave me a book of Jesus' own writing to encourage me the more freely to come; and he said concerning that book, that every word and letter thereof stood firmer than heaven and earth. Then I asked him what I must do when I came; and he told me I must entreat on my knees, with all my heart and soul, the Father to reveal Him to me. Then I asked him further how I must make my prayer to Him; and he said, Go, and thou shalt find Him upon a mercy-seat, where He sits all the year long to give pardon and forgiveness to them that come. I told him that I knew not what to say when I came; and he bid me say to this effect: God be merciful to me a sinner, and make me to know and believe in Jesus Christ; for I see that if His righteousness had not been, or I have not faith in that righteousness, I am utterly cast away. Lord, I have heard that Thou art a merciful God, and hast given that Thy Son Jesus Christ should be the Saviour of the world;

and, moreover, that Thou art willing to bestow Him upon such a poor sinner as I am. And I am a sinner indeed. Lord, take therefore this opportunity, and show Thy grace in the salvation of my soul, through Thy Son Jesus Christ. Amen.

Christian: And did you do as you were bidden?

Hopeful: Yes, over, and over, and over.

Christian: And did the Father show His son to you?

Hopeful: Not at the first, nor second, nor third, nor fourth, nor fifth; no, nor at the sixth time neither.

Christian: What did you do then?

Hopeful: What! why, I could not tell what to do.

Christian: Had you no thoughts of leaving off praying?

Hopeful: Yes; a hundred times twice told.

Christian: And what was the reason you did not?

Hopeful: I believed that that was true which had been told me; to wit, that without the righteousness of this Christ, all the world could not save me; and therefore, thought I with myself, if I leave off I die, and I can but die at the throne of grace. And withal, this came into my mind: 'Though it tarry, wait for it; because it will surely come, it will not tarry.' So I continued praying until the Father showed me His Son.

(Christian and Hopeful Speak of Faithful's Preaching, *The Pilgrim's Progress*)

A humble and poor tinker, often incarcerated, untrained in the art of preaching, unlicensed to pastor, and without a proper education, became one of the most important Baptists, and, indeed, Christians, to ever live. John Bunyan's role in the Puritan and Nonconformist affairs of the seventeenth century will forever be etched in Church history, joining the great cloud of witnesses of biblical and church heroes of faith spoken of in the Valhalla-like halls of the Hebrews 11 Hall of Faith. But Bunyan was a pastor before he was an activist and, though acknowledged in many places, it is being forgotten in the twenty-first century that Bunyan was lauded in his day for his exceptional *preaching*.

We have already spent some time becoming acquainted with the Tinker and his life through his writings. But, let's now pause to turn an eye back to some of his writings and most momentous occasions to learn who the Tinker was as a preacher of God's Word.

Yes, as an author of an incredible body of works (including the phenomenally popular *Pilgrim's Progress*), pursuer of piety and godliness, and pastor of Bedforshire, Bunyan is rightly remembered alongside the Pauls, Augustines, Luthers, and Calvins of the Christian faith. Yet, despite his immense popularity, it was his ability as an expositor of Scripture that made it possible for him to excel in these other areas. This exceptional ability in preaching the Scriptures was developed within a framework of firm and unwavering Baptistic convictions.

His ministry was so powerfully impactful *because* of his preaching, and not at all hindered by it. In fact, a short foray once more into his compelling life-story will reveal that the power of his preaching and writing lay within its simplicity, which was peculiar to the Particular Baptists and Puritans, and wielded with exceptional depth by Bunyan due to his own personal experiences with conversion, suffering, and replete joy in the Lord.

This chapter will aim to once more trace the historical context in which Bunyan ministered to better understand his extraordinary ability to articulate, through preaching and writing, the deepest truths of the Christian faith. To do so, his simplistic yet passionate way of explaining grand doctrinal truths will be examined in light of his own conversion experience (explored in depth already in previous chapters), wherein it was the simple declaration of truth that led to his embracing the gospel. Secondly, an examination into the role that suffering played in Bunyan's life will be undertaken so that a line may be drawn between his own experiences and ability to speak into the pain and suffering of his listeners and readers. Finally, this chapter will give attention to Bunyan's biblical insights by understanding how the Bible, and Baptistic convictions, influenced every sphere of his thought and life.

Simple, Passionate, Soul-Winning Preaching

John Owen, perhaps one of the greatest Puritan theologians, once made it a point to go and hear the preaching of the comparatively simple Bunyan. If Owen was like the Einstein of his day, Bunyan was like the science professor at a local community college: Both engaged in the same field of study, but one clearly the more academically respected of the two. Yet, when Owen was questioned by King Charles why he would go and visit the Tinker to hear his preaching, Owen responded that he would willingly trade his great learning to preach with an ability to touch men's hearts like Bunyan could.[1] Owen, despite his incredible intellect and learning, was amazed by Bunyan's preaching and recognized within the Tinker something that no amount of seminary training or academic knowledge can teach and no amount of money can buy: A true anointing of the Holy Spirit upon the preacher of God's Word.

This is not to say, however, that Bunyan was without intellect. On the contrary, though untrained like many of his peers, Bunyan possessed a sharp mind and Holy Spirit-filled heart that discerned the great truths of Scripture and preached them well to people. In fact, Bunyan was no slouch when it came to defending doctrinal perspectives amongst the more academically minded of his generation. As explained within *The Baptist Story*, 'In the 1670s Kiffen became embroiled in a controversy with John Bunyan over the necessity of believer's baptism... [Bunyan] rejected the standard Particular Baptist argument that believer's baptism must precede membership in the local church and the privileges of that membership, particularly participation in the Lord's Supper.'[2] Bunyan wrote a few works about this topic during the controversy. In fact,

---

1. John Piper, 'To Live Upon God That Is Invisible: Suffering and Service in the Life of John Bunyan,' *Desiring God*, Sermon preached February 2, 1999, https://www.desiringgod.org/messages/to-live-upon-god-that-is-invisible.

2. Anthony L. Chute, Nathan A. Finn, and Michael A. G. Haykin, *The Baptist Story: From English Sect to Global Movement* (Nashville: B&H Academic, 2015), 46.

within one such work, *A Confession of My Faith, and A Reason of My Practice*, Bunyan introduces the topic by explaining, within both the subtitle and introduction paragraph, that he was setting forth a defense of the fact that he 'By diverse argument, that though I dare not communicate with the openly profane, yet I can with those visible Saints that differ about water-baptism. Wherein is also discoursed, whether that be the entering ordinance into fellowship, or no.'[3] While the Tinker would not participate in spiritual communion with the openly wicked and profane, he did find unity with regenerate believers, even if they did not share his Baptistic distinctives. This work sets forth his argument for allowing open communion and, though one may certainly disagree with his conclusions, he defended each part of his doctrinal beliefs with Scripture, with which one must contend if they wish to disagree.

These works prove Bunyan was not lacking in intelligence or wisdom but show that his preaching and writing were both simple by design and, thus, all the more powerful and impactful. This may be attributed, first, to his being untrained in a seminary setting. He was an anomaly even among Nonconformists—whereas many possessed knowledge of Greek and Hebrew, Bunyan possessed none. Yet, he possessed that highly sought-after treasure that all Christian men and women desire: a true knowledge of the living God which permeated both head and heart. Considering the volume of Bunyan's corpus, and the number of topics he penned books on, it is evident that the Lord blessed him with a keen intellect and capable mind. After all, only one who is intelligent can make great truths easy to understand to all. So, while his lack of training may have produced simplistic expositions of Scripture, it seems fair to believe that Bunyan also conscientiously chose to preach in a way understandable by learned theologians and common lay people alike.

His preaching style is on display in his wonderful work, *The Saints' Knowledge of Christ's Love*, where, in explaining Ephesians 3:18-19 (which states, '[so that you] may have

---

3. Bunyan, *A Confession of My Faith, and a Reason of My Practice, Works*, (Edinburgh, UK: Banner of Truth, 1991), 2:593.

strength to comprehend with all the saints what is the breadth and length and height and depth, and to know the love of Christ that surpasses knowledge, that you may be filled with all the fullness of God...'[ESV]) he writes:

> Breadth, and Length, and Depth, and Height, are words that in themselves are both ambiguous, and to wonderment; ambiguous, because unexplained, and the wonderment, because they carry in them an unexpressible something; and *that* something that which far out-goes all those things that can be found in this world... They are here... to suggest to us the unsearchable infinite greatness of God; who is *breadth*, beyond all breadths; a *length*, beyond all lengths; a *depth*, beyond all depths; and a *height* beyond all heights, and that in all his attributes: He is an eternal being, an everlasting being, and in that respect he is beyond all measures, whether they be of breadth, or length, or depth, or height.[4]

This is typical of Bunyan's writing. He both explains the theological truth of a particular text and then immediately applies it into the context of his readers and listeners so that, by beholding the greatness and glory of the Triune God, they might be brought to their knees in praise of Him. This is the essence of simplicity in preaching and experiential faith. Not only did Bunyan teach the great doctrines of the faith, but he also made them easy to understand and applicable for everyday life.

Bunyan earnestly desired for both his listeners and readers to know Christ in the same way that he did, and he never seemed to forget how God had first revealed Himself to the sinful Tinker. As Bunyan's autobiography title, *Grace Abounding to the Chief of Sinners*, makes clear, he, like the Apostle Paul, saw himself as the worst of all sinners and recipient of the greatest of all graces: salvation in Jesus. That message was central to all his preaching and writing. Beyond this, Bunyan always remembered that he was led to Christ partially through the providential encounters he had with his first wife and her books, like 'Arthur Dent's *The Plain Man's Pathway to Heaven*

---

4. Bunyan, *The Saints' Knowledge of Christ's Love, Works*. 2:3.

and Lewis Bayly's *The Practice of Piety*,'[5] and also with the town's foul-mouthed woman rebuking him for his own filthy language. Perhaps even some of his humor is on display when he writes of this latter encounter, 'though she was a very loose and ungodly wretch, yet protested that I swore and cursed at that most fearful rate... That I was the ungodliest fellow for swearing that ever she heard in all her life; and that I, by thus doing, was able to spoil all the youth in a whole town, if they came but in my company.'[6] This was not the holy rebuking the ungodly, but the ungodly rebuking one even more ungodly still. Bunyan personally knew the power of conviction in the heart of a sinner called to repent by another sinner, which was something he often did in his sermons thereafter.

This encounter had a profound effect on his own awareness of sin; an effect so grand, it evidently left a lasting impression upon him and appears to have encouraged him in preaching repentance of sin to others. Though Bunyan appears to have possessed some humor in his preaching as he did in his writing, he also possessed a Holy Spirit-driven sobriety in his calling sinners to repentance. However, it was that latter group of women who, in utter and astonishing joy, spoke simply of the salvation they had experienced in Christ that compelled him to draw near to Christ himself, and would become an indelible mark of his own ministry. In his writing, he explains how they spoke of the New Birth, 'how God had visited their souls with his love in the Lord Jesus, and with what words and promises they had been refreshed, comforted, and supported against the temptations of the devil.'[7] He did not understand their words in their fulness just yet, but they were attractive to the sinner now looking for forgiveness in Christ. These same matters would later permeate the preaching and writing of the Tinker. The gospel would have been incomplete if he did not both call sinners to repentance *and* to trust in Jesus for everlasting life and joy.

5. Joel R. Beeke and Randall J. Pederson, *Meet the Puritans* (Grand Rapids: Reformation Heritage Books, 2006), Kindle Edition Loc. 1809.

6. Bunyan, *Grace Abounding to the Chief of Sinners*, *Works*, 1:9.

7. Ibid., 10.

These latter women were incredibly instrumental in not only leading Bunyan to Christ, but in shaping his future ministry. Not only was their joy infectious in that Bunyan desired to experience it himself, but their simple way of explaining the faith of the gospel was encouraging to the restless heart of the sinful man. Is it any surprise his later preaching was marked by profound joy and simply explained gospel truths? Soon, the women seized the opportunity to introduce Bunyan to their own pastor. Joel Beeke records that, 'In 1651, the women introduced Bunyan to John Gifford, their pastor in Bedford. God used Gifford to lead Bunyan to repentance and faith. Bunyan was particularly influenced by a sermon Gifford preached on Song of Solomon 4:1… as well as by reading Luther's commentary of Galatians…'[8] God utilized the simple words of these women, a simple sermon from a pastor, and the simple words of a book to lead Bunyan to salvation. Finally, the conversion of his soul was itself experienced when, 'While walking through a field one day, Christ's righteousness was revealed to Bunyan's soul and gained the victory.'[9]

That simplicity through which Christ was made known to him would be a distinguishing mark of his own preaching and writing in his attempts to make Christ known to others. Perhaps this is no clearer than in his preface to *Good News for the Vilest of Men*, wherein he writes, 'One reason which moved me to write and print this little book was, because, though there are many excellent heart-affecting discourses in the world that tend to convert the sinner, yet I had a desire to try this simple method of mine; wherefore I make bold thus to invite and encourage the worst to come to Christ for life.'[10] His method was to simply call all to repent and trust in Jesus. But Bunyan was marked by more than just simplicity; his life was also one of suffering.

The Influence of Suffering in Bunyan's Ministry

From the beginnings of the Baptist movement, it was obvious that they composed the most 'Nonconformist' bunch of the

---

8. Beeke and Pederson, *Meet the Puritans*, Loc. 1817-1824.

9. Ibid.

10. Bunyan, *Good News for the Vilest of Men*, *Works*, 1:68.

Nonconformist lot. Despised and hated by many, including their other Puritan and Nonconformist brethren, they often found themselves on the receiving end of mockery, punishment, and suffering.

Almost all the Particular Baptists of the seventeenth century understood suffering well and, often, found themselves threatened, beaten, imprisoned, and left for dead for both their Protestant faith and Baptistic convictions. John Bunyan was no exception. The man was imprisoned at least twice and spent over a decade of his life imprisoned for his insistence on continuing to preach the gospel without a license from within the church of England.

Contemporaries and especially successors of Bunyan have long recognized how God used suffering in his life to mold him into a great Christian. Indeed, *Pilgrim's Progress,* and its many allegories of suffering in the Christian life, is a pure example of how Bunyan's years spent in prison and experiencing religious intolerance and persecution shaped his thought. George Whitefield, the great revivalist preacher, picked up on this aspect of Bunyan's life and preached that this was an example of how God utilizes suffering to increase the effectiveness of His people in bringing glory to His name. John Piper quotes Whitefield as having said of *The Pilgrim's Progress,* 'It smells of the prison. It was written when the author was confined in Bedford jail. And ministers never write or preach so well as when under the cross: the Spirit of Christ and of Glory then rests upon them.'[11]

Most of Bunyan's corpus has this aroma about it. This was not merely a man who wrote from ivory towers about how a Christian could best learn to endure suffering for God's glory; this was a man who had suffered immensely for the sake of the gospel, the Kingdom of God, and patiently endured all for the glory of the Lord. His heart's desire was to pass this learning on to other believers who would suffer persecution for their faith.

Perhaps the clearest example of his desire to impart wisdom about suffering (next to the allegorical nature of *Pilgrim's*

---

11.   John Piper, 'To Live Upon God That Is Invisible: Suffering and Service in the Life of John Bunyan,' *Desiring God.*

Progress, of course), is his *Prison Meditations.* Structured in simplistic, yet beautiful, poetry, Bunyan writes:

> Though men do say, we do disgrace
> Ourselves by lying here
> Among the rogues, yet Christ our face
> From all such filth will clear.
>
> We know there's neither flout nor frown
> That we now for him bear,
> But will add to our heavenly crown,
> When he comes in the air.
>
> When he our righteousness forth brings
> Bright shining as the day,
> And wipeth off those sland'rous things
> That scorners on us lay.
>
> We sell our earthly happiness
> For heavenly house and home;
> We leave this world because 'tis less,
> And worse than that to come.
>
> We change our drossy dust for gold,
> From death to life we fly;
> We let go shadows, and take hold
> Of immortality.[12]

Bunyan's heart was that suffering for Christ was worth it because, if the gospel was being preached, Christ was being glorified. All persecutors of God's people would be brought under God's judgment. And, ultimately, the benefits of serving and following Christ far outweighed all benefits that may have been afforded by the world.

This language was only possible because Bunyan, like the Apostle Paul, had learned the secret of contentment in all situations. Like Paul in Philippians 4:11-13, he could say, 'I have learned in whatever situation I am to be content. I know how to be brought low, and I know how to abound. In any and every circumstance, I have learned the secret of facing plenty and hunger, abundance and need. I can do all things through him who strengthens me' (ESV). Because Bunyan had

---

12. Bunyan, *Prison Meditations, Works,* 1:65.

received a great outpouring of grace from Christ, it seemed little trouble to spend over a decade in prison for the sake of Christ and His Kingdom.

Bunyan was surrounded by disease, war, famine, and persecution. As Joel Beeke and Paul Smalley write, 'A historian remarks that Bunyan saw "the most turbulent, seditious, and factious sixty years of recorded English history." Bunyan himself lost his first wife and spent more than twelve years in prison. His personal life was full of hardship, persecution, and suffering.'[13] Wars and rumors of wars surrounded the Tinker. He saw his Puritan brethren persecuted and knew that, like the Magisterial Reformers a century prior, his lot in life was to fight for Reformation, even if it meant his own death. And, indeed, Bunyan experienced a great deal of suffering during his life.

He fought as a soldier in the Parliamentary ranks. He and his first wife, Mary, were quite poor. Their first daughter, and eldest of his six children, was born blind. His first wife passed away and Bunyan was soon imprisoned after marrying his second wife, Elizabeth. Over a decade younger than the thirty-one-year-old Tinker, she experienced a miscarriage while her husband was in prison, as she tried to fight for his release. While Bunyan could have been released if he had merely agreed to stop preaching without a license, he could not, in good conscience, stop preaching the Word of God, nor could he agree to seek licensure within a church body he vehemently opposed with his Puritan convictions. Eventually, Bunyan would die on 31 August, 1688, after a bout of illness due to exposure.

From his arrest onward, trials plagued the Bunyans. As explained within *The Baptist Story*, 'On November 12, 1660, authorities arrested Bunyan as he was about to preach in Lower Samsell, a hamlet near Harlington, Bedfordshire. Tried and convicted under the Elizabethan Conventicle Act of 1593, Bunyan spent most of the next twelve years in prison.'[14] Yet, even in this, the Tinker had his eyes on Christ. Bunyan later

---

13. Joel R. Beeke and Paul M. Smalley, *John Bunyan and the Grace of Fearing God* (Phillipsburg: P&R Publishing, 2016), 1.

14. Anthony Chute, Nathan A. Finn, and Michael A. G. Haykin, *The Baptist Story: From English Sect to Global Movement* (Nashville: B&H Academic, 2015), 42-43.

claimed, 'The subject I should have preached upon, even then when the constable came, was, "Dost thou believe on the Son of God?" From whence I intended to shew, the absolute need of faith in Jesus Christ; and that it was also a thing of the highest concern for men to inquire into, and to ask their own hearts whether they had it or no.'[15] This message did not change while he was imprisoned; rather, the message became stronger. 'Bunyan's imprisonment proved to be the catalyst for developing his gifts as an author. Here he wrote his powerful apology for nonconformity, *I Will Pray with the Spirit* (1662), as well as a rebuttal of antinomianism, *Christian Behaviour* (1663), along with his classic *Grace Abounding to the Chief of Sinners* (1666); the latter went through six editions in his lifetime.'[16] By the grace of God, suffering imprisonment allowed for the Tinker to focus on writing some of the greatest contributions to Christian literature.

Encouraging others in suffering finds its way into much of Bunyan's writing. When preaching and writing on Acts 24:14-15, for example, and expositing the doctrine of the resurrection, Bunyan recorded in *The Resurrection of the Dead and Eternal Judgment*, 'Whence note by the way, that a hypocritical people, will persecute the power of those truths in others, which themselves in words profess. I have hopes toward God, and that, such a hope which themselves do allow, and yet I am this day, and that for this very thing, persecuted by them.'[17] While this work continually encourages Christians to look forward to the resurrection as the eternal hope and weight of glory prepared for the saints of God in the midst of trials and sufferings, he does not shy away from his own experience with suffering and persecutions either. He saw the divine hand of God providentially tracing the course of his allotted days and understood that, whatever suffering he experienced, God had either ordained or allowed it to take place. Therefore, he could trust all the suffering of his life was ordained by the merciful hand of God for a purpose and a reason; namely, to glorify His own name and edify His saints.

---

15. Bunyan, *A Confession of My Faith, and a Reason of My Practice*, *Works*, 2:593.

16. Chute, Finn, and Haykin, *The Baptist Story*, 42-43.

17. Bunyan, *The Resurrection of the Dead and Eternal Judgment*, *Works*, 2:85.

It was, perhaps, this firsthand experience with persecution and suffering that made Bunyan's writings and preaching so impactful and visceral to his readers and listeners. This was not a man merely engaged in thinking about suffering, but a man of God who had truly gone through the furnace and found the fourth man, Jesus, to eternally be by his side. Lesser men may have crumpled beneath the trials, temptations, and persecutions. This is not to suggest Bunyan was superhuman, but that he possessed a sustaining and persevering grace from the Lord in the face of trials. Ultimately, his endurance in suffering and ability to draw from his own experiences to teach others was the result of himself having been completely molded by Scripture. The Word of God had permeated every area and sphere of his thought and life so that even difficulties like great suffering could not be understood apart from Scripture.

The Bible-Saturated Thought of Bunyan

This is the most important quality that the Tinker possessed: an indefatigable knowledge of and love for Scripture.

Any amount of time spent with Bunyan will be time profitably spent with the Bible. This is because Bunyan constantly quotes Scripture directly or alludes to it in a variety of ways. Even in his allegorical writings, Scripture is clearly on his mind. To understand Bunyan, one must have an open Bible nearby to frequently consult. As Charles Spurgeon once said of Bunyan. '"Why, this man is a living Bible!" Prick him anywhere—his blood is Bibline, the very essence of the Bible flows from him. He cannot speak without quoting a text, for his very soul is full of the Word of God. I commend his example to you, beloved.'[18] Knowing that 'So faith comes from hearing, and hearing through the word of Christ' (Rom. 10:17 ESV), it should be little surprise that the man who frequently quotes the Word of God in all his writings should

---

18.   Charles Spurgeon, 'Mr. Spurgeon as a Literary Man,' in *The Autobiography of Charles H. Spurgeon*, Compiled from His Letters, Diaries, and Records by His Wife and Private Secretary, vol. 4, 1878-1892 (Curtis & Jennings, 1900), 268. https://www.thegospelcoalition.org/blogs/justin-taylor/do-you-bleed-bibline/

have such a large impact on the spread of the gospel among the heathen and the edification of the saints.

Take, for example, just the opening sentences of *Pilgrim's Progress* and the inclusion of Scripture: "'I saw a man clothed with rags, standing in a certain place, with his face from his own house, a book in his hand, and great burden upon his back," (Isa. 64:6. Luke 14:33. Ps. 38:4. Hab. 2:2. Ac. 16:31.)'[19] Just this opening section alone has attached to it five different texts from the Bible, each taken from a different book, some in the Old Testament and some in the New Testament. This sort of scriptural influence is found throughout the entire allegory. Bunyan was so well-versed in Scripture that it had, evidently, permeated his pores, thoughts, and soul. As Spurgeon said, one may have pricked the man and not been surprised to discover he bled Bible.

Bunyan may have lacked the academic and seminary training possessed by many of his contemporaries, but what he lacked in formal education, he made up for in personal study and devotion. He was one who had done all he could do to present himself as one approved before God, 'a worker who [had] no need to be ashamed, [who] rightly [handled] the word of truth' (2 Tim. 2:15 ESV). The Word of God was his constant, and sometimes only, companion over a lifetime of great suffering.

Combined with his own conversion experience, where the gospel of Jesus Christ's death, burial, and resurrection was simply and clearly made real to him, and his own experience with almost constant sorrow, his biblical influence made his preaching and writing more impactful than perhaps any other preacher or writer, outside of the biblical authors themselves. God, in His sovereignty and divine providence, saw fit to take a simple Tinker, transform him into a Christian saved by grace alone, and use him as a simple preacher and writer of amazing biblical and doctrinal truths.

Bunyan's encouragement to modern Christians is as straightforward as the man's preaching was. Christians today must constantly remember that it was the simple gospel message of a glorious Savior, Jesus Christ, that saved

---

19. Bunyan, *The Pilgrim's Progress*, *Works*, 3:89.

our sinful souls. Great grace has been shown to great sinners. It is this same grace that will carry us all the way home to Christ, through tribulations, persecutions, and sufferings; yea, even through the valley of the shadow of death itself. Bunyan teaches us that grace carries us and Christ leads us. Therefore, like Bunyan, we ought to continually read, study, delight in, and meditate on Scripture. It was both his experiences and knowledge of these truths that made his life so very impactful, and these same truths must continue to teach Christians today, especially in the midst of great trials and suffering.

CHAPTER 8

The Tinker Called Home to the Celestial City:
The Final Days of Bunyan

And he said, 'This river has been a terror to many; yea, the
thoughts of it have also frighted me; but now methinks I
stand easy; my foot is fixed upon that on which the feet of
the priests that bare the ark of the covenant stood while
Israel went over Jordan. The waters, indeed, are to the
palate bitter, and to the stomach cold; yet the thought of
what I am going to, and of the conduct that waits for me on
the other side, doth lie as a glowing coal at my heart. I see
myself now at the end of my journey; my toilsome days are
ended. I am going to see that head which was crowned with
thorns, and that face which was spit upon for me. I have
formerly lived by hearsay and faith; but now I go where I
shall live by sight, and shall be with Him in whose company
I delight myself. I have loved to hear my Lord spoken of;
and wherever I have seen the print of His shoe in the earth,
there I have coveted to set my foot too. His name has been
to me as a perfume box; yea, sweeter than all sweet smells.
His voice to me has been most sweet, and His countenance
I have more desired than they that have most desired the
light of the sun. His Word I did use to gather for my food,
and for medicine against my faintings. He has held me,

and hath kept me from my sins; yea, my steps hath He
strengthened in His way.'

Now, while he was thus speaking, his countenance changed,
his strong man bowed under him; and, after he had said,
'Take me, for I come unto Thee!' he ceased to be seen
of them.

But glorious it was to see how the open region was filled
with horses and chariots, with trumpeters and pipers, with
singers and players on stringed instruments to welcome the
pilgrims as they went up, and followed one another in at the
beautiful gate of the City.

(The Pilgrims Enter the Celestial City, *The Pilgrim's Progress,*
Part Two)

John Bunyan's earthly pilgrimage came to an end on 31 August,
1688. He was almost sixty years old. He had fallen ill while on
a journey to act as a peacemaker between a father and son in
Reading and it was here, on his way back home, that he was
called home to be with his Lord. Imagine the celebration that
must have taken place as the Tinker entered the celestial city!

But that is not to say his final days were without importance.
On the contrary, even as he entered his fifth decade of life,
the Tinker showed no signs of slowing down. Only ten years
prior, after all, during his second prison stay, he had written
The Pilgrim's Progress, and it went through a total of eleven
editions, in the successive years of 1678 to 1685, and again in
1688. Likewise, the second part of *The Pilgrim's Progress* went
through at least two editions in 1684 and 1686, respectively.

Two other allegorical tales were written during this time,
including *The Life and Death of Mr Badman* in 1680 and *The Holy
War* in 1682. Even after his death, a few more of his works
would be posthumously published with the help of Elizabeth
Bunyan. Clearly, had the Lord seen fit to allot the Tinker more
time on earth, then he would have written even more works.
In fact, he ended the second part of *The Pilgrim's Progress* by
writing of Christian's sons, 'Shall it be my lot to go that way
again, I may give those that desire it an account of what I here

am silent about: meantime I bid my reader Adieu.'[1] Evidently, he had at least entertained the idea of writing further tales about the descendants of Christian the Pilgrim.

So, in what would unexpectedly become his final days on earth, how did Bunyan spend his time?

Clutching Sinners from the Flames of Hell and Fighting for the Truth While Tinkering with Books

Unsurprisingly, Bunyan took part in two important tasks after his imprisonment and during those final years of his life: He preached and wrote to spread the gospel and see souls saved, and he took part in controversies, doing his best to defend the deep truths of the Word of God against those who would attack them.

The last year of his life was as productive as ever. He published an impressive six works, and had two others completed, before he passed away. It is staggering to think of how many works he may have published if given only another ten years to keep working.

Consider his *The Jerusalem Sinner Saved*, or *Good News for the Vilest of Men*. This work was published in the year of his death and really encapsulates both the man and the theology he held so dear. It is the work of a gifted evangelist who passionately and earnestly longs to see lost sinners united to Christ by faith. The genuine warmth from the Tinker toward the lost is prevalent throughout, but so too is his adamant call for sinners to repent and believe the gospel. His writing, which is equally as strong as it is warm, is a window into his heart.

Read this plea from the Tinker toward the sinner, and see if you cannot help but hear his pleas with them vocalized in your own ears:

> When thou art called to an account for thy neglects of so great salvation, what canst thou answer? or dost thou think that thou shalt escape the judgment? (Heb 2:3). No more such Christs! There will be no more such Christs, sinner! Oh, put not the day, the day of grace, away from thee! if it be once gone, it will never come again, sinner.

---

1. John Bunyan, *The Pilgrim's Progress (The Second Part)*, *Works*, 3:241.

But what is it that has got thy heart, and that keeps it from thy Saviour? 'Who in the heaven can be compared unto the Lord? who among the sons of the mighty can be likened unto the Lord?' (Psa 89:6). Hast thou, thinkest thou, found anything so good as Jesus Christ? Is there any among thy sins, thy companions, and foolish delights, that, like Christ, can help thee in the day of thy distress? Behold, the greatness of thy sins cannot hinder; let not the stubbornness of thy heart hinder thee, sinner.

Objection. I am ashamed.

Answer. Oh! don't be ashamed to be saved, sinner.

Objection. But my old companions will mock me.

Answer. Oh! don't be mocked out of eternal life, sinner.

Thy stubbornness affects, afflicts the heart of thy Saviour. Carest thou not for this? Of old, 'he beheld the city, and wept over it.' Canst thou hear this, and not be concerned? (Luke 19:41,42). Shall Christ weep to see thy soul going on to destruction, and will though sport thyself in that way? Yea, shall Christ, that can be eternally happy without thee, be more afflicted at the thoughts of the loss of thy soul, than thyself, who art certainly eternally miserable if thou neglectest to come to him. Those things that keep thee and thy Saviour, on thy part, asunder, are but bubbles; the least prick of an affliction will let out, as to thee, what now thou thinkest is worth the venture of heaven to enjoy.[2]

The entire work follows a pattern very similar to this. Bunyan explains the gospel and the need of the sinner to turn to Christ in repentance and faith, without delay, for a salvation instantaneous, sure, and secure. Then, having lived for years in vanity and pride, making many of his own objections to Christ and His gospel, raises the objections he foresees the sinner making and then answers those objections in such a sure way that the sinner is left without any reason, whatsoever, to reject Christ any longer. Instead, they are compelled

---

2. John Bunyan, *The Jerusalem Sinner Saved*, or *Good News for the Vilest of Men*, *Works*, 1:90.

to come to Christ for forgiveness of sins and to enjoy an eternal salvation.

His final sermon preached at London includes a similar style. This sermon, preached 19 August, 1688, was delivered at Gamman's meetinghouse, which was near Whitechapel. The text he exposited was John 1:13, 'Which were born, not of blood, nor of the will of the flesh, nor of the will of man, but of God.' He closed that final sermon with the following application:

> Make a strict inquiry whether you be born of God or not. Examine by those things I laid down before of a child of nature and a child of grace. Are you brought out of the dark dungeon of this world into Christ? Have you learned to cry, My Father? (Jer. 3:16), 'And I said, Thou shalt call me thy Father.' All God's children are criers. Can you be quiet without you have a belly full of the milk of God's word? Can you be satisfied without you have peace with God? Pray you consider it, and be serious with yourselves. If you have not these marks, you will fall short of the kingdom of God, you shall never have an interest there; there is no intruding. They will say, 'Lord, Lord, open to us; and he will say, I know you not.' No child of God, no heavenly inheritance. We sometimes give something to those that are not our children, but not our lands. O do not flatter yourselves with a portion among the sons, unless you live like sons. When we see a king's son play with a beggar, this is unbecoming; so if you be the king's children, live like the king's children. If you be risen with Christ, set your affections on things above, and not on things below. When you come together, talk of what your Father promised you; you should all love your Father's will, and be content and pleased with the exercises you meet with in the world. If you are the children of God, live together lovingly. If the world quarrel with you, it is no matter; but it is sad if you quarrel together. If this be amongst you, it is a sign of ill-breeding, it is not according to rules you have in the Word of God.[3]

This was the attitude that compelled Bunyan to continue preaching during these later years. After the success of his works, and especially *The Pilgrim's Progress*, the Tinker had become something like a celebrity of his day. It would have been easy to simply coast off the relative success of this works

---

3. Bunyan, *Mr. Bunyan's Last Sermon*, *Works*, 2:757-58.

and never write or preach another word again. But this was not in his character. He was a hard worker, especially when it came to the service of Christ and His Kingdom.

For these same reasons, he was willing to engage in lofty theological debates in his final years. While it would have been even easier to not engage himself in the effort of debating those whom he had found to be wanting in their explanation of the doctrines of Scripture, he instead readily took up the pen to do theological battle with those whose doctrines he found most troublesome.

Questions About the Nature and Perpetuity of the Seventh-Day Sabbath is one such work. Published in 1685, Bunyan takes to the Scriptures to prove that the right practice of the Sabbath has moved from the final day of the week (Saturday) to the first day of the week (Sunday), as this is the day that Christ rose from the grave.

He explains, in his letter to the reader, that he is quite aware that the majority of orthodox Christians, for many centuries, had already believed the Sabbath was now to be kept on Sundays. However, he explains, 'I have observed that some, otherwise sound in faith, are apt to be entangled with a Jewish sabbath, etc., and that some also that are afar off from the observation of that, have but little to say for their own practice, though good; and might I help them I should be glad.'[4]

Bunyan's goal hardly seems to have been to make a name for himself, or to puff himself up. Rather, even in theological debates, his goal was always to lead others into truth. For this reason, Bunyan rarely offers any new or novel theological concepts or ideas. His insistence on declaring only the truth prohibited him from inventing new and strange doctrines. To his credit as well, knowing what we do of the man, it appears safe to say that if someone could have shown him in Scripture where he had gotten one doctrine or another wrong, he gladly would have repented and changed his mind.

His final years were spent in much the same way. Preaching and writing to see sinners saved and the children of God led

---

4. Bunyan, *Questions About the Nature and Perpetuity of the Seventh-Day Sabbath*, *Works*, 2:361.

into truth, warring against those perverse doctrines that threatened the glory of Christ.

A Nation's Return to Rome?

Fear spread among the Protestants, and especially the Nonconformists, when in 1685, Charles II died. While the Protestants were not large fans of much that he had done, his brother was a leader they certainly did not want to see wear the crown because he was a Roman Catholic. James II would, despite Puritan fears, become king, and panic would soon spread.

The Duke of Monmouth launched a failed revolution in fear of England once more falling prey to Roman Catholicism. Even Bunyan, who typically displayed great courage, thought that James II spelled disaster for himself and his family. Therefore, on 23 December, 1685, he signed a deed which transferred possession of all that he owned to his wife. Now, if he would be imprisoned again or executed by a tyrannical Roman Catholic king, at least his family would be provided for.

However, that persecution did not fall upon the Tinker. Instead, Bunyan was able to voice some of his political opinion, which would effectively protect both his family and future generations from a return to the monolithic structure of the Roman Catholic Church in the lead up to the Protestant Reformation. Beeke and Smalley explained:

> In 1687, an agent of the king reported that he had interviewed the 'Pastor to the Dissenting Congregation' in Bedford, and Bunyan had declared his support 'for electing only such members of Parliament as will certainly vote for repealing all the Tests and penal-Laws touching Religion.' Evidently Bunyan treasured liberty of conscience, even though it would also open a door for Roman Catholicism in England, a religion that Bunyan strongly opposed as Babylon and Antichrist.[5]

---

5. Joel R. Beeke and Paul M. Smalley, *John Bunyan and the Grace of Fearing God* (Philipsburg: P&R Publishing, 2016), 27.

Preaching the Word of the Lord Until Called Home by the Lord

Bunyan had been warned against going to Reading in Berkshire to act as a reconciler between the estranged father and son. He was no longer the rambunctious young man he had once been. He was now nearing sixty and had spent a good portion of his life imprisoned in the Bedford jail. While he was not the unhealthiest of men around, those years of persecution and imprisonment had certainly taken their toll. Besides, George Offor notes that he was also suffering from what was known as 'the sweating sickness,' which was 'as fatal as cholera.'[6]

Was any person truly surprised, however, when he refused to rest? This was the same man who, when offered a lighter jail sentence if only he would quit preaching, refused the lighter sentence, and openly declared before his judges, 'If you let me go, I will immediately go out and preach again.' Obviously, he was going to go and do what he could to make peace between father and son. This was who he was, after all, at heart. His calling was that of tinker: A mender of both pots and pans and the hearts of men.

The trip was deemed a success, and the two men were reconciled to one another. Mission accomplished, Bunyan made his way back home from Reading, traveling through London. While traveling on horseback, he met with heavy rains which played some part in the fever which then struck him. It appears this was either on 19 August, 1688, or slightly before, and he still managed to preach his final sermon while in London on that day. (Perhaps this is the reason for the brevity of this final sermon.)

While in London, he was able to stay with a dear friend, a Mr. John Strudwick. But recovery would not take place. A stroke would follow, and it would become clear that his final days had come. Bedford was about two days' journey from London at this time, and this left the Tinker without the comfort of his poor wife for some days.

---

6. Offor, *Memoir of John Bunyan*, *Works*, 1:lxxiii.

Even facing death, Bunyan remained the steadfast saint he had been since conversion. With eyes fixed on Jesus, he desired to encourage those around him. George Offor recorded that his final words were: 'Weep not for me, but for yourselves. I go to the Father of our Lord Jesus Christ, who will, no doubt, through the mediation of his blessed Son, receive me, though a sinner; where I hope we ere long shall meet, to sing the new song, and remain everlastingly happy, world without end. Amen.'[7]

Praise the Lord, this is exactly where Bunyan has been since his passing on 31 August, 1688; in the loving and tender embrace of Christ, where we who have called upon Jesus Christ as Lord and Savior shall one day be as well.

He was, initially, buried at the back of the Bunhill Fields Burial Ground, in a section called the 'Baptist Corner.'[8] An arrangement was made with Strudwick for his remains to be removed into the Strudwick family vault at some point in the future when the tomb was opened again. Probably, this move occurred in 1695, when Strudwick himself died. Though an exact date for the moving of the remains is unknown, the vault, shaped like a Baroque chest, bore an inscription for both the Strudwick family and John Bunyan himself. Over the next two centuries, the vault would fall into a sad state of disrepair.

In the second part of *The Pilgrim's Progress*—which is unfortunately the lesser-known sequel to the original—the events that transpired after Christian made his way to the celestial city are recorded. In speaking of Christian's current estate in the celestial city, Mr. Sagacity declares:

> Besides, it is confidently affirmed concerning him, that the King of the place where he is has bestowed upon him already a very rich and pleasant dwelling at court, Zech. iii.7; and that he every day eateth, Lu. xiv.15, and drinketh, and walketh, and talketh with him; and receiveth of the smiles and favours of him that is Judge of all there. Moreover, it is expected of some, that his Prince, the Lord of that country, will shortly come into these parts, and will know the reason, if they can give any, why

---

7. Ibid.

8. Robert Philip, *The Life, Times and Characteristics of John Bunyan, author of the Pilgrim's Progress* (London: Thomas Ward, 1839), 578.

his neighbours set so little by him, and had him so much in derision, when they perceived that he would be a pilgrim, Jude 14, 15. For they say, that now he is so in the affections of his Prince, and that his Sovereign is so much concerned with the indignities that were cast upon Christian, when he became a pilgrim, that he will look upon all as if done unto himself; and no marvel, for it was for the love that he had to his Prince that he ventured as he did. Lu. x.16.[9]

The same, as Bunyan wrote of Christian, could now be said of himself. He had entered into the embrace of his tender, compassionate, powerful, and loving Savior. Jesus Christ will indeed right all wrongs just as surely as He has rewarded the Tinker for his earthly service to the Kingdom of God.

The Tinker finished his course well. Let's look to him as an example that we too may someday say, 'I have fought a good fight, I have finished my course, I have kept the faith: Henceforth there is laid up for me a crown of righteousness, which the Lord, the righteous judge, shall give me at that day: and not to me only, but unto all them also that love his appearing' (2 Tim. 4:7-8).

---

9. Bunyan, *The Pilgrim's Progress (The Second Part)*, *Works*, 3:172.

CHAPTER 9

The Lasting Legacy of the Tinker: Practical Applications from His Life

As I walked through the wilderness of this world, I lighted on a certain place where was a Den, and I laid me down in that place to sleep: and, as I slept, I dreamed a dream. I dreamed, and behold...

(The opening to *The Pilgrim's Progress*)

On 21 May, 1862, Charles Spurgeon unveiled the restoration of John Bunyan's tomb to the world. Located still in Bunhill Fields Burial Ground, London, the tomb was no longer secluded in the 'Baptist Corner,' but placed openly for all visitors to see. Created by the sculptor Edgar George Papworth Senior, the Baroque Chest shape of the vault was kept, but now a sculpted figure (known as a tomb effigy) of Bunyan was carved and placed on top, as though sleeping. On two of the sides, panels were added to depict scenes from *The Pilgrim's Progress*.

The tomb is not as glamorous as it would have been at that public unveiling. It was restored again in 1928, marking the tricentennial anniversary of Bunyan's birth. Evidently, further restorations had to be made after World War II, due to war time damages further desecrating the tomb. Today, the time and wear of weather and age has painted the formerly white tomb with countless imperfections. But, one can still clearly make out the words, 'JOHN BUNYAN, Author of the Pilgrim's Progress, OBT 31st AUGT 1688, AET[1] 60.'

It was at this unveiling that Spurgeon had the opportunity to speak, nearly two hundred years after the death of the Tinker, of his own profound impact on the Prince of Preachers. In the preface to *Pictures from Pilgrim's Progress*, Spurgeon's son, Thomas Spurgeon, wrote:

> The language of The Illustrious Dreamer was to the mind of the Tabernacle Pastor. They spake the same tongue. In an address delivered in 1862 on the occasion of the restoration of Bunyan's tomb, Mr. Spurgeon assured his hearers that Bunyan's works would not try their constitutions as might those of Gill and Owen. 'They are pleasant reading,' said he, 'for Bunyan wrote and spoke in simple Saxon, and was a diligent reader of the Bible in the old version.'[2]

The Prince of Preachers found, within the Tinker, an Immortal Dreamer whose writings and allegories were rare within the contours of history as pieces of literature that transcended time and culture. It was not that Bunyan's contemporaries were unexceptional,[3] but that the Tinker was exceptionally gifted by God's grace to reach all people, of all places, with the simple truths of the gospel.

Let each of us, now, look to the Tinker and be reminded, 'Wherefore seeing we also are compassed about with so great a cloud of witnesses, let us lay aside every weight, and the sin which doth so easily beset us, and let us run with patience the race that is set before us, Looking unto Jesus the author and finisher of our faith; who for the joy that was set before him

---

1. AET is an abbreviation meaning, 'At the age of.' Bunyan died at the age of 60.

2. Thomas Spurgeon, *Preface*, Charles Spurgeon, *Pictures from Pilgrim's Progress: A Commentary on Portions of John Bunyan's Immortal Allegory* (Grace e-books, http://www.grace-ebooks.com/library/Charles%20Spurgeon/CHS_Pictures%20From%20Pilgrims%20Progress.PDF), 4-5.

3. Far from it. John Owen, John Gil, Jonathan Edwards, Thomas Goodwin, and many others were also fantastic examples of Reformed, Puritan, experiential, doxological Christianity.

endured the cross, despising the shame, and is set down at the right hand of the throne of God' (Heb. 12:1-2).

In this chapter, I will aim to outline several lessons that I have learned from the Tinker and his life, which I hope and pray the reader will learn as well.

1. The Tinker proves that God calls whomsoever He will to accomplish His works.

God does not need a single person to accomplish His works upon the earth. He is sovereign and, as Paul preached in Acts 17:25, 'Neither is worshipped with men's hands, as though he needed any thing, seeing he giveth to all life, and breath, and all things.'

If God so desired, He could accomplish every one of His plans and works without the use of a single human being. However, according to His great mercy and grace, God has chosen to accomplish His purposes through secondary means, and He often uses people as the means to accomplish His purposes.

Take, for example, the preaching of the gospel. God has elected a number of people to salvation, and those people will most assuredly be saved. But God has chosen to accomplish the salvation of the elect through the preaching of the gospel. For this task, an evangelist is needed.

> For whosoever shall call upon the name of the Lord shall be saved. How then shall they call on him in whom they have not believed? and how shall they believe in him of whom they have not heard? and how shall they hear without a preacher? And how shall they preach, except they be sent? as it is written, How beautiful are the feet of them that preach the gospel of peace, and bring glad tidings of good things! (Rom. 10:13-15).

What a great gift from the Lord that, unworthy and unprofitable though we be, He has elected to use us, mere sinners saved by grace, to go forth and proclaim the great grace of the gospel now to others! Of course, we cannot save a single soul; God does that. Our success is not dependent on the number of souls we see saved, but on our faithfulness to the gospel message itself. But, the fact that God calls us to preach His gospel to others is amazingly wonderful!

Yet, how often do excuses pile up in the hearts of saints? They make excuses, claiming they could not possibly be expected to preach to anyone at any point. After all, they aren't as learned as some, they say. Or, they're just not very good at speaking. Or, they have no real ability to do so. And, with many other excuses, they try to feign an inability to do what God has commanded.

Such excuses ought not to be named amongst God's elect! When the Lord calls us to do something, we must do it, trusting that He will supply the sufficient grace we need to do it, just as he did for the Tinker.

John Bunyan was the least likely of all saints to be used to reach the world. He was the son of a tinker, perhaps descended from gypsies, with a poor education. Yet, God used him to write some of the greatest works in the English language, still being read today. *The Pilgrim's Progress* alone is still one of the most read works of all time.

Likewise, he was used to preach to an incredible number of people simply because he was willing to go and preach to those peoples. It has been estimated by Charles Doe within *The Struggler*:

> When Mr. Bunyan preached in London, if there were but one day's notice given, there would be more people come together to hear him preach than the meeting-house would hold. I have seen to hear him preach, by my computation, about twelve hundred at a morning lecture, by seven o' clock, on a working day, in the dark winter time. I also computed abut three thousand that came to hear him one Lord's-day, at London, at a town's end meeting-house; so that half were fain to go back again for want of room, and them himself was fain, at a back door, to be pulled almost over people to get upstairs to his pulpit.[4]

It was not his learning, high position in society, or social graces that made the crowds flock to hear the Tinker preach. Rather, it was his simple proclamation of gospel truths and warm Christian love that attracted so many to him.

---

4. Charles Doe, *The Struggler*, within *Works*, 3:766-67.

If God was able to use Bunyan, He most certainly can use you.

2. The Tinker encourages us to be students of the Word of God.

Throughout the years of his uncertainty regarding assurance of salvation, he continually returned to the Scriptures. He knew that, if he would ever find assurance, it must come through God's inerrant Word. Over time, he learned to love the Bible.

When imprisoned, it was once again the Scriptures that became his constant companion. He had nowhere else to turn. In a prison cell, by himself, his encouragement came through the study of Scripture. He would later become so certain of his learning of the Word of God, that he challenged readers to search the Scriptures to see if the doctrines he taught were true. He wrote in the preface to *Light for Them That Sit in Darkness*:

> Reader, let me beseech thee to hear me patiently; read, and consider, and judge. I have presented thee with that which I have received from God; and the holy men of God, who spake as they were moved by the Holy Ghost, do bear me witness. Thou wilt say, All pretend to this. Well, but give me the hearing, take me to the Bible, and let me find in thy heart no favour if thou find me to swerve from the standard...
>
> I have not writ at a venture, nor borrowed my doctrine from libraries. I depend upon the sayings of no man. I found it in the Scriptures of truth, among the true sayings of God.[5]

To say that Bunyan knew Scripture *well* would be an understatement. It is better to say, as others have, that if the man was pricked, he would have bled Bible. Even just a glimpse at *The Pilgrim's Progress* reveals hundreds of Scripture references—they fill almost every page! And, not only do Scripture references abound, but in his allegorical works, each of the scenes he created involves some interpretation of Scripture.

---

5. Bunyan, *Light for Them That Sit in Darkness*, *Works*, 1:392-93.

As he matured in Christ, he learned to love the Word of God all the more, and the more he learned to love the Word, the more he matured in Christ. Let every one of us, looking to Bunyan, be encouraged to obey the Apostle's teaching in 2 Timothy 2:15, 'Study to shew thyself approved unto God, a workman that needeth not to be ashamed, rightly dividing the word of truth.'

3. The Tinker teaches us to be a people of prayer.

Perhaps it should be of little surprise that the man that admired Martin Luther so much was also a man that entrenched his life in prayer. It was Luther who once quipped, 'I have so much to do today, I best pray for at least three hours first,' and Bunyan was one to follow suit.

Grace Abounding reveals that the nature of his prayer life was one of deep and profound seriousness. He was willing, like Jacob, to wrestle with the Lord in prayer to get the answers that he sought. On other occasions, it seems nearly possible that the great drops of sweat may have fallen from the Tinker while he prayed, so serious was he about bringing his needs and requests before the Lord.

In *Mr. John Bunyan's Dying Sayings*, there are a few pieces of wisdom on prayer that encapsulate his entire teaching on prayer in the life of Christian:

> In all your prayers forget not to thank the Lord for his mercies. When thou prayest, rather let thy hearts be without words, than thy words without a heart. Prayer will make a man cease from sin, or sin will entice a man to cease from prayer. The spirit of prayer is more precious than treasures of gold and silver. Pray often, for prayer is a shield to the soul, a sacrifice to God, and a scourge for Satan.[6]

As Paul wrote in Philippians 4:6-7, 'Be careful for nothing; but in every thing by prayer and supplication with thanksgiving let your requests be made known unto God. And the peace of God, which passeth all understanding, shall keep your hearts and minds through Christ Jesus.'

---

6. Bunyan, *Mr. John Bunyan's Dying Sayings, Works*, 1:65.

4. The Tinker teaches us to be steadfast saints for Christ and His Kingdom.

There were many instances where Bunyan could have denied Christ or, at the very least, denied his calling to preach the Word of God. But he refused. He would stand for Christ and His Kingdom, even if it meant suffering cruel and unusual punishments at the hands of men.

One of my favorite pieces from any of Bunyan's writings is found within *The Holy War*, when the king's son, Emmanuel, is appointed to conquer the town of Mansoul as the captain of their salvation:

> Wherefore the King called to him Emmanuel, his Son, who said, 'Here am I, my Father.' Then said the King, 'Thou knowest, as I do myself, the condition of the town of Mansoul, and what we have purposed, and what thou hast done to redeem it. Come now, therefore, my Son, and prepare thyself for the war, for thou shalt go to my camp at Mansoul. Thou shalt also there prosper and prevail, and conquer the town of Mansoul.'
>
> Then said the King's Son, 'Thy law is within my heart: I delight to do thy will. This is the day that I have longed for, and the work that I have waited for all this while. Grant me, therefore, what force thou shalt in thy wisdom think meet; and I will go and will deliver from Diabolus, and from his power, thy perishing town of Mansoul. My heart has been often pained within me for the miserable town of Mansoul; but now it is rejoiced, but now it is glad.'
>
> And with that he leaped over the mountains for joy, saying, 'I have not, in my heart, thought anything too dear for Mansoul: the day of vengeance is in mine heart for thee, my Mansoul: and glad am I that thou, my Father, hast made me the Captain of their salvation. And I will now begin to plague all those that have been a plague to my town of Mansoul, and will deliver it from their hand.'[7]

At this point in the narrative, those in the court who hear of the son being appointed to go and deliver Mansoul begin to rejoice. They also desire to join the war effort themselves,

---

7. Bunyan, *The Holy War*, *Works*, 3:284.

counting it a most just war and worthwhile cause, to follow the son into battle to save Mansoul.

This exchange, though simple, gets at the heart of the story that we have been called to be a part of. Jesus, our triumphant and conquering King, has an eternal Kingdom and possesses all rule and authority. At Calvary, Jesus both defeated sin and Satan, publicly putting the devil to open shame (Col. 2:13-15). Now, Jesus is in the business of plundering Satan's domain (Matt. 12:29), and this is the work that we join in together with Him when we stand steadfast for Him and His Kingdom.

Let us learn from Bunyan's own steadfastness to be steadfast ourselves for Christ, and to stand upon the promises of Scripture, for the Lord has promised, 'Of the increase of his government and peace there shall be no end, upon the throne of David, and upon his kingdom, to order it, and to establish it with judgment and with justice from henceforth even for ever. The zeal of the LORD of hosts will perform this' (Isa. 9:7). Let us have faith to believe that our work for Christ matters eternally and that He will accomplish His most perfect purposes.

5. The Tinker reveals that those who have godly fear are the most joyful in Christ.

Grace Abounding to the Chief of Sinners is, in my own estimation, one of the greatest writings ever produced by man and, if a Christian will only ever read one of Bunyan's works, it should be this one. But reading it can also be an exercise in patience. Lord willing, the chapter in this work on his conversion was able to convey this well enough, but one must really read his own autobiography to get a feel for how deep Bunyan's uncertainties and anxieties ran.

Yet, when Bunyan finally found true assurance of salvation in Christ, not every fear departed. One fear remained, and of this fear we may say that it is the most important for all man to possess, for it is the proper fear of God.

Bunyan wrote of the fear of God, 'For there is no duty performed by us, that can by any means be accepted of God, if it be not seasoned with godly fear.'[8]

---

8. Bunyan, *A Treatise on the Fear of God*, *Works*, 1:438.

He knew the importance of godly fear, but this should not be taken to mean that he was without joy. In fact, he knew that no matter the trial, hardship, or situation he found himself in, because he possessed Christ and Christ possessed him, he could always have the utmost joy.

There is a wonderful scene in *The Pilgrim's Progress* when Christian and Hopeful are in the dungeon of Doubting-Castle when, suddenly, Christian exclaims:

> 'What a fool,' quoth he, 'am I to lie in a foul-smelling dungeon, when I may as well walk at liberty! I have a key in my bosom called Promise, that will, I am sure, open any lock in Doubting Castle.' Then said Hopeful, 'That is good news, good brother: pluck it out of thy bosom, and try.'
>
> Then Christian pulled it out of his bosom, and began to try at the dungeon door, whose bolt, as he turned the key, gave back, and the door flew open with ease, and Christian and Hopeful both came out.[9]

The point of this scene is that, for the believer in Christ, there is no despair that can hold us down for long. Rather, because we know the author and finisher of our salvation (Heb. 12:2) we can rejoice continually (Phil. 4:4).

6. The Tinker teaches us how to suffer persecution well.

Bunyan knew the horrors of persecution, the trials of tribulation, and the pain of suffering. He lost his mother and sister in close proximity to one another. His first daughter was born blind. His first wife passed away. He was often the target of terrible acts of slander. For twelve years, he was imprisoned for preaching the gospel.

His *Prison Meditations* are helpful for those in the bonds of affliction. In meditations five through seven, he wrote:

> I am, indeed in prison now
> In body, but my mind
> Is free to study Christ, and how
> Unto me he is kind.
> For though men keep my outward man

---

9. Bunyan, *The Pilgrim's Progress, Works*, 3:142-43.

> Within their locks and bars,
> Yet by the faith of Christ I can
> Mount higher than the stars.
> Their fetters cannot spirits tame,
> Nor tie up God from me;
> My faith and hope they cannot lame,
> Above them I shall be.[10]

Bunyan, having gone through the fires of affliction, comforts us with the comforts found in Christ alone. Let men do what they will to us; not one thing happens apart from our sovereign Lord's notice. But, the best news of all, is that no one and no thing is able to pluck us from the hands of Christ (John 10:28-29) and no one or thing can separate us from God's love which we now possess in Christ (Rom. 8:31-39). Storms and trials may come. Deep suffering, such as imprisonment, may be God's plan and portion for our lives as it was for Bunyan. Seasons come and seasons go, but our Lord does not change, 'his compassions fail not. They are new every morning: great is thy faithfulness' (Lam. 3:22-23).

Looking to Bunyan, we can suffer well for the cause of Christ because we know the vast comforts of Christ.

7. The Tinker teaches us the importance of dreaming.

Bunyan's preaching and writing were gifts of God's grace, but so too was his imagination. Many, in fact, believed that when he opened *The Pilgrim's Progress* by suggesting that he was recounting a dream, or vision, he had been given, he meant he really did dream the whole story and then put pen to paper. In reality, he simply had the imagination needed to write the story.

While his allegorical writings and poetry are some of the best examples of his imaginative and winsome nature, the truth is that all his writings, and sermons, bear the mark of one who was a dreamer. His imagination allowed him to create art (in his writings) for the great and supreme glory of God. Likewise, this same imagination allowed him to contrive of great illustrations within his sermons that granted his

---

10. Bunyan, *Prison Meditations, Works*, 1:64.

listeners and readers great understanding and insight into the truths of Scripture he was preaching and outlining for them. Some reading this may think that they lack the prowess to create anything worthwhile for God and His Kingdom. On the contrary, if the Tinker could do it—and he was the least likely of all creatures to create works of art—then most certainly the one reading this can as well.

Those preachers reading this will also benefit from the use of their imagination. I do not mean that you should invent meanings within the text. No, let Scripture be its own interpreter and you preach that interpretation. But, when you prepare your sermons, imagine the congregation that will listen and think, 'What sort of illustrations might I provide that would best explain this text?' Or, 'How does this text speak directly to the hearts of the listeners? Are there any problems, right now in their lives, that this text can address?' Questions like these appear to have always been at the forefront of Bunyan's mind.

It was this imagination, employed for the use of glorifying God, that would later reach even the Prince of Preachers himself, Charles Spurgeon, with the gospel. In his early days, 'He came upon the illustrations in Bunyan's *Pilgrim's Progress*. "When I first saw in it the woodcut of Christian carrying the burden on his back I felt so interested in the poor fellow that I thought I should jump for joy when, after he had carried it so long, he at last got rid of it."'[11] Imagine it! Bunyan himself scarcely could have thought his little allegorical work would, nearly two centuries later, influence one of the greatest Christian preachers to ever walk the earth. Who can say, but God, how your own works and efforts may be used by the Lord to bless the saints of future generations?

Use your imagination, in whatever way God has equipped you, to preach and proclaim the simple truths of the gospel, make works of art to bring glory to our Triune God, and dream that you might bless the saints.

---

11. Arnold Dallimore, *Spurgeon: A Biography* (Edinburgh, UK: The Banner of Truth Trust, 1985), 6.

Onward, Christian Pilgrims

More lessons can certainly be learned from Bunyan's life. But I suggest you find some of his works and begin to read them yourself. They are a rich treasure trove of ancient truths, warm comforts, and plain teachings of deep theological wisdom.

John Bunyan was a wonderful man of God who lived all of his life for all of Christ. He sought to glorify the Lord always and found that his own joy was directly proportional to the amount of glory he was bringing to Christ through his life. But he was a flawed man. He did not have perfect theology—who does?—and he was not without sin. Yet, we can learn from him, and this we must do. Do not worship the man, but learn from him and his life to become a more mature Christian.

Above all else, the Tinker teaches us to look to Jesus Christ. We, as Christians, are pilgrims on a journey to the celestial city. The Tinker completed his journey because his eyes were fixed firmly on Christ. So, let us follow in his own footsteps and set our eyes upon Jesus, who is the author and finisher of our faith.

Onward, Christian Pilgrims.

BIBLIOGRAPHY

Beeke, Joel R. and Paul M. Smalley. *John Bunyan and the Grace of Fearing God*. Philipsburg: P&R Publishing, 2016.

Beeke, Joel R. and Randall J. Pederson. *Meet the Puritans*. Grand Rapids: Reformation Heritage Books, 2006. Kindle Edition.

Brittain, Vera. In the Steps of John Bunyan: An Excursion into Puritan England. London, UK: Rich and Cowan, 1950.

Bunyan, John. *The Works of John Bunyan*. Edited by George Offor. 3 vols. 1854. Reprint, Edinburgh, UK: Banner of Truth, 1991. Works cited from these volumes include:

A Confession of My Faith, and a Reason of My Practice

A Treatise on the Fear of God

A Vindication of Gospel Truths Opened

Christian Behaviour

Come and Welcome to Jesus Christ: A Plain and Profitable Discourse on John 6:37

Differences in Judgment about Water Baptism, No Bar to Communion

Good News for the Vilest of Men

Grace Abounding to the Chief of Sinners

Light for Them That Sit in Darkness

Mr. Bunyan's Last Sermon

Mr. John Bunyan's Dying Sayings

Questions About the Nature and Perpetuity of the Seventh-Day Sabbath

Relation of Bunyan's Imprisonment

Scriptural Poems

Some Gospel Truths Opened

The Doctrine of Law and Grace Unfolded

The Holy War

The Jerusalem Sinner Saved

The Law and Grace Unfolded

The Pilgrim's Progress

The Resurrection of the Dead and Eternal Judgment

The Saints' Knowledge of Christ's Love

Calvin, John. *Institutes of the Christian Religion.* Trans. Henry Beveridge. Peabody, MA: Hendrickson Publishers, 2008.

Carlton, Charles. *Going to the Wars: The Experience of the British Civil Wars, 1638-1631.* London, UK: Routledge, 1992.

Chute, Anthony L., Nathan A. Finn, and Michael A. G. Haykin. *The Baptist Story: From English Sect to Global Movement.* Nashville: B&H Academic, 2015.

Dallimore, Arnold. *Spurgeon: A Biography.* Edinburgh, UK: The Banner of Truth Trust, 1985.

de Lisle, Leanda. *The White King: Charles I, Traitor, Murderer, Martyr.* New York: Hachette Book Group, 2017. Kindle Edition.

Denne, Henry. *THE QUAKER NO PAPIST, in Answer to The Quaker Disarm'd. OR, A brief Reply and Censure of Mr. Thomas Smith's frivolous Relation of a Dispute held betwixt himself and certain Quakers at Cambridge.* London, 1659. https://ota.bodleian.ox.ac.uk/repository/xmlui/bitstream/handle/20.500.12024/A81304/A81304.html?sequence=5&isAllowed=y

Doe, Charles. *The Struggler.* 1680. (Printed within Vol. 3 of *The Works of John Bunyan.* 1854. Reprint, Edinburgh, UK: Banner of Truth, 1991.)

Gifford, John. *Preface* to John Bunyan's *A Few Sighs from Hell.* 1658. (Printed within Vol. 3 of *The Works of John Bunyan.* 1854. Reprint, Edinburgh, UK: Banner of Truth, 1991.)

Luther, Martin. *Luther's Works.* Ed. and trans. Theodore G. Tappert. Vol. 54, *Table Talk.* Philadelphia: Fortress Press, 1967.

Murray, Iain H. *Sermons of the Great Ejection.* Edinburgh, UK: The Banner of Truth Trust, 1962.

Offor, George. *Memoir of John Bunyan.* 1854. (Printed within Vol. 1 of *The Works of John Bunyan.* 1854. Reprint, Edinburgh, UK: Banner of Truth, 1991.)

Offor, George. *Preface* to *The Works of John Bunyan.* 1854. (Printed within Vol. 1 of *The Works of John Bunyan.* 1854. Reprint, Edinburgh, UK: Banner of Truth, 1991.)

Ó Siochrú, Micheál. 'Atrocity, Codes of Conduct and the Irish in the British Civil Wars 1641-1653.' Past & Present 195:1 (2007).

Payne, Lynda. 'Health in England (16th–18th c.),' in Children and Youth in History, Item #166. https://chnm.gmu.edu/cyh/items/show/166. (Accessed December 2, 2021.)

Philip, Robert. *The Life, Times and Characteristics of John Bunyan,* author of the Pilgrim's Progress. London: Thomas Ward, 1839.

Piper, John. 'To Live Upon God That Is Invisible: Suffering and Service in the Life of John Bunyan,' *Desiring God/* Sermon preached February 2, 1999. https://www.desiringgod.org/messages/to-live-upon-god-that-is-invisible.

Powell, Vavasor. 'To Christ our King.' Found within Alexander Griffith, *Strena Vavasoriensis,: a Nevv-Years-gift for the Welch itinerants, or a hue and cry after Mr. Vavasor Powell, metropolitan of the itinerants, and one of the executioners of the Gospel, by colour of the late Act for the propagation thereof in Wales; as also a true relation of his birth, course of life, and doctrines; together with a vindication of several places of Scripture wrested and abused, against the present government, and all publick ministers of this nation. His hymn sung in Christ-Church London; with an antiphona there unto; and a lively description of his propagation.* London: F.L., 1654. https://quod.lib.umich.edu/e/eebo2/A8 5696.0001.001/1:4?rgn=div1;view=fulltext

Simson, James. *Was John Bunyan a Gipsy?.* New York: James Miller, 1882. Accessed through Project Gutenberg.

Spurgeon, Charles. 'Mr. Spurgeon as a Literary Man,' in *The Autobiography of Charles H. Spurgeon,* Compiled from His Letters, Diaries, and Records by His Wife and Private Secretary. Vol. 4,1878-1892. Curtis & Jennings, 1900. As quoted in: https://www.thegospelcoalition.org/blogs/justin-taylor/do-you-bleed-bibline/

Spurgeon, Thomas. *Preface* to Charles Spurgeon's *Pictures from Pilgrim's Progress: A Commentary on Portions of John Bunyan's Immortal Allegory.* Grace e-books. http://www.grace-ebooks.com/library/Charles%20Spurgeon/CHS_Pictures%20From%20Pilgrims%20Progress.PDF

Thomson, Andrew. *Life of John Owen,* in *Works of John Owen Vol. 1.* 1850. Reprint, Edinburgh, UK: Banner of Truth Trust, 1965.

Venables, Edmund. *The Life of John Bunyan*. Walter Scott, 1888. Reprint, Project Gutenberg Edition, 2005.

Whitefield, George. *Works*, IV. London, 1771. Quoted within: J.I. Packer. *A Quest for Godliness: The Puritan Vision of the Christian Life*. Wheaton, Il: Crossway, 1990.

Woodbridge, John D. and Frank A. James III. *Church History Volume Two: From Pre-Reformation to the Present Day*. Grand Rapids: Zondervan, 2013.

The Heavenly Footman: How to Get to Heaven
by John Bunyan

Throughout Bunyan's great allegories his prime concern was that people would be able to discern the way to heaven. The 'Footman' is an athlete dogged in the pursuit of 'winning' the race.

Bunyan wants us to be able run the race of the Christian life and finish the course so that we might all meet in Heaven. As he states in this book:– 'Farewell, I wish our souls may meet with comfort at the journey's end.'

Based on the text 'so run that ye may obtain' (1 Cor. 9:24), Bunyan's terse and racy style gives us vital guidance on how to complete the journey. This is regarded as one of the classic texts to have come from the Puritan era on Christian living. Bunyan is well known for his perceptiveness in describing human motivation and thought processes with discernment as he gives us the 'description of the man who gets to heaven.'

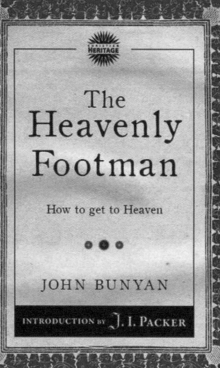

The
Heavenly
Footman

How to get to Heaven

● ● ●

JOHN BUNYAN

INTRODUCTION BY J. I. PACKER

Christian Focus Publications

Our mission statement –

STAYING FAITHFUL

In dependence upon God we seek to impact the world through literature faithful to His infallible Word, the Bible. Our aim is to ensure that the Lord Jesus Christ is presented as the only hope to obtain forgiveness of sin, live a useful life and look forward to heaven with Him.

Our books are published in four imprints:

CHRISTIAN FOCUS

Popular works including biographies, commentaries, basic doctrine and Christian living.

CHRISTIAN HERITAGE

Books representing some of the best material from the rich heritage of the church.

MENTOR

Books written at a level suitable for Bible College and seminary students, pastors, and other serious readers. The imprint includes commentaries, doctrinal studies, examination of current issues and church history.

CF4•K

Children's books for quality Bible teaching and for all age groups: Sunday school curriculum, puzzle and activity books; personal and family devotional titles, biographies and inspirational stories – because you are never too young to know Jesus!

Christian Focus Publications Ltd,
Geanies House, Fearn, Ross-shire,
IV20 1TW, Scotland, United Kingdom.
www.christianfocus.com